Power and Personality In Speaking

POWER AND PERSONALITY IN SPEAKING

G. Kleiser

The Readers Paradise
New Delhi

POWER AND PERSONALITY IN SPEAKING

Ist Indian Edition, 2017
Reprint - 2018, 2019, 2023

ISBN - 978-93-85958-52-6

Published by
The Readers Paradise
103, 4787/23, Ansari Road,
Darya Ganj, New Delhi - 110002
Phone: 011-23246222, 23246333
Mobile : 09811197091, 9654444181
e-mail : thereadersparadisesales@gmail.com
Website - www.thereadersparadise.com

Price - Rs. 499.00

Type Setting
Sanya Computers

Printed in India
Balaji Offset

Preface

Every man seeks power. It may be social, financial, or political power, physical, mental, or spiritual power, according to the ideal he sets before him. The highest and most enduring power is that which comes from the development of personal character.

The purpose of this book is to give practical suggestions and exercises for building the body, the voice, and the vocabulary, for training the memory and imagination, and for the general development of power and personality in the speaker.

The author's work as instructor in public speaking has brought him into intimate touch with the needs of men of widely varied type and temperament. He has observed in many instances the lack of development in these two essentials to true success—power and personality—and it is his hope that this book will help many men to realize more fully their highest ideals.

In conjunction with this work the author has compiled, in ten small volumes, "The World's Great Sermons," which will be found useful in solving many problems of right living.

Appreciative acknowledgment is made to authors and publishers for kind permission to use copyrighted material.

Author

Introduction

We have here an elucidation that is thoroughly sane of the art of expression by one who has made himself master of his task by careful study and training as a teacher of students of preaching. Professor Kleiser is quite right in his opinion that ministers "have not yet come to realize to any appreciable extent the value of thorough training in the art of expression." The writer is able to confirm this judgment by many years of experience as a teacher of homiletics. There is doubtless a well-grounded prejudice against certain methods of teaching "elocution" so called that have prevailed in time past. But intelligent preachers and students of the art of preaching should know, and in fact do know, that such methods are obsolescent and that modern methods of teaching the art of expression are rational and normal.

The task that every public speaker has to master is the task of handling himself. No man can accomplish that task without thorough training in the art of expression, and every student of his art should be eager to avail himself of the best that can be done for him in securing such thorough and facile handling of himself. "What we need," says Emerson, "is vent" But this depends on the kind of vent.

Untrained vent, like that of a wild locomotive that has lost control of its forces and has left the rails, is of little avail. Training in a normal method of expression will not fail to have a reactionary effect upon the activities of the mind as well as upon the emotions, the imagination and the will. Such training enables one to coordinate the products of the mind with the emotional and ethical activities.

What a man says is not the speaker's entire problem, and in and for itself alone is after all not the supreme interest. The literary and artistic form of thought is part of its very life, and the form which speech takes in vocal utterance and in the manifestation of other forces of the physical personality is proportionately important. A preacher's delivery is the transmission of his message through the potencies of his personality. It is the expression of himself, and at its best it must be the trained self. It is the speaker's method of uttering to best advantage the physical, mental, emotional and moral forces of his personal being. The free normal expression and interpretation of great truth is a genuine inspiration which every preacher should know. It is not a credit to any man's intelligence, and much less to his moral purpose, that he treats with contempt so important an art as that which would train his personality as the organ of religion and would equip him for the expression of its great realities with dignity, grace and strength. The dramatist spares himself no toil in the culture of self-expression. His success depends upon it.

Preaching is an art, but it is a moral art, and on moral grounds the preacher should train himself assiduously and laboriously in the exercise of it.

Professor Kleiser has done well to direct attention once more, and in so forceful, attractive and practical a manner, to the importance of the art of which he is at once the master and the servant. It is to be hoped that through this volume he may secure new incentive to the study of this art, and that he may find the realization of his most ardent desires.

Lewis O. Brastow

Contents

1 Power and Personality in Speaking

The public speaker and the preacher have much in common. The difference lies mainly in their message. Both are concerned with the problem of convincing and persuading men. To achieve this result there must be brought to bear the highest possible training in thought and expression.

In the best sense, a public speaker should be a man of sterling character, of lofty purpose, of trained ability, and, like the preacher, he should be prepared, if need be, to offer himself a living sacrifice in the cause of truth. "Let no man who is a sneak try to be an orator," said Beecher, and he might have added, Let no man aspire to distinction in public speaking, whether in pulpit, on platform, or elsewhere, unless he be willing to spend his days and nights in developing all the resources of his mind, voice, and body.

The lawyer can learn much from the sincerity, sympathy, and persuasiveness of the preacher; the preacher in turn may take a valuable lesson from the concise, direct, and convincing style of the lawyer; while the average public speaker may learn from both the value of truth and earnestness as effective elements in speech.

Assuming that the preacher, thoroughly trained in

voice and manner, having the highest truth to proclaim, and uttering it from a position of authority, is the ideal public speaker, may we not here find the fundamental elements of success for those who would speak with truth and effectiveness upon other occasions?

Two essential elements in successful preaching are truth and personality. By truth here is meant God's revelation. The truth of the preacher is the Bible truth. Not exclusively, for the Bible will conduct him beyond the Bible, to the heart, to history, and to the book of nature, but the ultimate authority for him is the Bible as the revealed truth of God. Three things are involved in this matter of truth—receiving, adapting, and giving. The preacher will first find and appropriate the truth to himself. He will adapt it in such a way as to make it available for his practical work as a teacher. He will adopt the best means in his power of giving that truth to others.

No one thing will add so much to a man's power in speaking as the conscious possession of truth. As Cardinal Newman says, "What is so powerful an incentive to preaching as the sure belief that it is the preaching of the truth?" The speaker knows he stands upon a solid rock, and this assurance produces the highest type of self-confidence.

It is the work of the preacher to interpret the truth, not to create it. That he may search out the right kind of truth he should have a clear and definite purpose ever before him. Phillips Brooks says, in speaking of the minister: "He must receive the truth as one who is to teach it. He can not, he must not study as if the truth he sought were purely for his own culture or enrichment This will bring, first, a deeper and more solemn sense of responsibility in the search for truth; second, a desire to find the human side of every truth, the point at which every speculation touches humanity; and, third, a breadth which comes from the constant presence in the mind of the fact that truth has various aspects and presents itself in many to different people, according to their needs and characters."[1]

It will be seen, then, that no two men will convey their message exactly alike. They will speak out of the fullness of their own hearts and experiences. Each man has a grasp of partial truth, but no man has the whole truth. As Professor James says, the truth is too great for any one actual mind. Each man will give what he has to give.

The importance of truth is nowhere emphasized more than in the Bible. "The *truth* of the Lord endureth forever."—*Psalm* cxvii., 2. "Thy law is the *truth.*"—*Psalm* cxix., 142. "All thy commandments are *truth.*"—*Psalm* cxix., 151. "He that walketh uprightly, and worketh righteousness, and speaketh the *truth* in his heart"—*Psalm* xv., 2. "All the paths of the Lord are mercy and *truth* unto such as keep his covenant and his testimonies."—*Psalm* xxv., 10. "His *truth* shall be thy shield and buckler."—*Psalm* xci., 4. "The lip of *truth* shall be established forever."—*Proverbs* xii., 19. "And ye shall know the *truth,* and the *truth* shall make you free."—*John* viii., 32. "Jesus saith unto him, I am the way, the *truth,* and the life: no man cometh unto the Father, but by me."—*John* xiv., 6. "Sanctify them through thy *truth:* thy word is *truth.*"—*John* xvii., 17. "For this cause came I into the world, that I should bear witness unto the *truth.* Every one that is of the *truth* heareth my voice."—*John* xviii., 37. "But speaking the *truth* in love, may grow up into him in all things, which is the head, even Christ."—

Ephesians iv., 15. "For the fruit of the Spirit is in all goodness and righteousness and *truth*."—*Ephesians* v., "Stand therefore, having your loins girt about with *truth* and having on the breastplate of righteousness."—*Ephesians* vi., 14. "And it is the Spirit that beareth witness because the Spirit is *truth*."—*I John*, v., 6.

The knowledge and consciousness of this truth will do much toward making a man eloquent in speech. "There is a calm and earnest trust in God's ordinance," says Austine Phelps, "that truth shall do its work in the salvation of men, which every preacher needs to make him what the world calls a natural orator. Possest of such a trust, all preachers may be natural orators. That trust creates the spirit of repose in the use of God's instrument It makes a preacher feel that he can afford to preach the truth naturally. He need not exaggerate it; he need not distord it; he need not deck it with meretricious ornament; he need not mince it, nor inflate it, nor paint it. He has only to speak it in a spirit of reverence and love, and let it do its work. I will do its work. He may safely repose in it. In the very heat and turmoil of the world's hostility to his message he may wrap himself in the spirit of a child's faith. That shall be to him and to his life's work like the mantle of prophet. He may *know* in his inmost soul that his word are the wisdom of God and the power of God."

But truth alone is not sufficient, else we might leave the sermon to the printed page. What is needed is the message and the man, or truth conveyed through personality. The qualities of a truly great personality are many. Among them are faith, personal piety, unselfishness, magnetism sociability, culture of mind and heart, and devotion the humanity. Paul's personality speaks even from the printed page because of his unquenchable love for men. The personal side of the preacher is strikingly emphasized by Beecher in his *Yale Lectures:* "Make religion attractive by the goodness that men see in you; be so sweet, so sparkling, so buoyant, so cheerful, hopeful, courageous, conscientious and yet not stubborn, so perfectly benevolent yet not mawkish or sentimental; blossoming in every that is good, a rebuke to everything that is mean or little—make such men of yourselves that everybody who looks upon you may say, 'That is a royal good fellow; he has the spirit that I should like to lean upon in time of trouble, or to be a companion with at all times.' Build up such a manhood that it shall be winning to men."

One great object of preaching, like other forms of public speaking, is persuasion. The final test is whether men act. They are convinced of the truth through the intellect; they are persuaded to act upon the truth through the heart. How this can best be done is one of the problems of successful preaching.

In his lecture on *The Secrets of Effective Preaching*[2] the Rev. J. H. Jowett says: "Months ago I determined that there should be more of the tender lover in my pulpit speech, more of the wooing note of the Apostle Paul, more of the gentleness and tender constraint of my Lord." He advocates less scolding and more pleading, less driving and more wooing in pulpit delivery. It is this tenderness of speech, the truth spoken in love, that wins men. Doctor Jowett further suggests that the preacher should question himself thus: "Do I feel sin to be loathsome? Am I possest of a tender sensitiveness, that can discern even the faintest movings in the hearts of my people, and which will reveal to me their inclinations long before they receive any outward expression? And, Lord Jesus, have I been a wooer, a lover, and are any in Thy kingdom because they were just enticed into it by the tender persuasiveness of my life and speech? And have I linked the proclamation of duties to the love of Calvary? And has my teaching had New Testament perspective and proportion, and have I evinced delight in my own message?"

The affectionate spirit in preaching is what is most needed. This will impart beauty and feeling to the spoken word. It will give zeal and sincerity to the message. Thus will the whole man speak when possest of the truth and a genuine love for men. Schleiermacher possest this "persuasive, penetrating, kindling effusion of feeling" in his preaching, and little do we wonder when we read these fervent words he wrote to his father: "From my heart I do wish that God's blessing may be upon my sermons, so that they may be sources of true edification and speak to the heart, as, I trust, they will ever come from the heart. To you I need not say how deeply I am moved at the thought of being numbered among those to whom so important an office is entrusted, nor need I assure you that I do not now, and never shall, look upon it merely as means of livelihood."

It is said of Cardinal Newman that the tones of his voice seemed as if they were something more than his own. His musical voice had such a rare charm for his hearers that they did not miss the entire absence of gesture. His body and soul glowed with suppress emotion as he entered more deeply into his subject. He is vividly described by Principal Shairp as having this peculiarity in delivery: "Each sentence was spoken rapidly, but with great clearness of intonation, and then, at the close of every sentence, there was a pause that lasted for several seconds. Then another rapidly but clearly spoken sentence, followed by another pause, till a wonderful spell took hold of the hearer. The look and bearing of the preacher were as of one who dwelt apart, and who, tho he knew his age well, did not live in his age. From his seclusion of study, and abstinence, and prayer; from habitual dwelling in the unseen, he seemed to come forth that one day of the week to speak to others of the things he had seen and known in secret. As he spake, how the old truths became new! how they came home with a meaning never felt before! The subtlest of truths were dropt out as by the way in a sentence or two of the most transparent Saxon. What delicacy of style, yet what calm power! how gentle yet how strong! how simple yet how suggestive! how homely yet how refined! how penetrating yet how tender-hearted! And the tone of voice in which all this was spoken sounded to you like a fine strain of unearthly music."[3]

Probably no American preacher is more closely studied than the late Phillips Brooks. He exemplified in his own life and preaching the force of a consecrated personality, which he so earnestly advocated to others. He claimed that the qualities most to be desired in the sermon—"clearness, logicalness, vivacity, earnestness, sweetness, and light"—should first be in the preacher himself, else they would not find their natural place in his message. Sincerity, courage, joy in one's work, purity and personal uprightness, he emphasized in his counsel to others and fully demonstrated in his own life. With his broad and genial optimism he said: "The world has not heard its best preaching yet. If there is more of God's truth for men to know, and if it is possible for the men who utter it to become more pure and godly, then, with both of its elements more complete than they have ever been before, preaching must some day be a complete power." Regarding Phillips Brooks himself, what higher tribute and recommendation can be offered to his honored name than these words of Doctor Brastow! "Any man who would know better what it is to be a helpful, pastoral preacher, a real preacher, full, simple, earnest, unconventional, the preacher of an imaginative, suggestive, and ethical mind, who cares chiefly to make the truth effective, who is bent upon getting it at work in the minds and hearts of men, who would fuse and fire the truth with the energies of a manly human soul, may well give himself with diligence to Phillips Brooks."[4]

The ultimate purpose of all true preaching is the salvation of men. The work of the Christian minister is the preaching of Christ and of Christianity as the one religion based on love. If his heart and tongue be not on fire with holy zeal in proclaiming this greatest of all gifts to man-kind, he can not and will not succeed. "Whenever a minister forgets," says Lyman Abbott, "the splendid message of pardon, peace, and power based on faith in Jesus Christ as God manifest in the flesh, whenever for this message he substitutes literary lectures, critical essays, sociological disquisitions, theological controversies, or even ethical interpretations of the universal conscience, whenever, in other words, he ceases to be a Christian preacher and becomes a lyceum or seminary lecturer, he divests himself of that which in all ages of the world has been the power of the Christian ministry, and will be its power so long as men have sins to be forgiven, temptations to conquer, and sorrows to be assuaged."[5]

A young man asked an old minister who had heard

him preach: "What do you think of my sermon?" "A very poor sermon, indeed," said he. "It took me a long time to prepare it," said the astonished young man. "Ay, no doubt of it" "Why, did you not think my explanation of the text a very good one?" "Oh, yes," said the old preacher, "very good, indeed." "Well, then, why do you say it is a poor sermon? Were not the metaphors appropriate, and the arguments conclusive?" "Yes, they were very good as far as that goes, but still it was a very poor sermon." "Will you tell me why you think it was a poor sermon?" "Because," said he, "there was no Christ in it" Said the young man: "Christ was not in the text; we are not to be preaching Christ always; we must preach what is in the text." The old minister said: "Don't you know, young man, that from every town and every village and every little hamlet in England, wherever it may be, there is a road to London? So from every text of Scripture there is a road to the metropolis of the Scriptures, that is, Christ And, my dear brother, your business is, when you get to a text, to say, 'Now what is the road to Christ?' and then preach a sermon, running along the road toward the great metropolis—Christ And I have never yet found a text that had not got a road to Christ in it, and if ever I do find one that has not got a road to Christ in it, I will make one; I will go over hedge and ditch, but I would get at my Master, for the sermon can not do any good unless there is a savor of Christ in it."

The essential elements, then, of successful preaching, and of any public speaking worth while, are truth and personality. The Christian preacher is at once an interpreter, a herald, a teacher, a counselor, an evangelist, an ambassador. His is the supreme message of life. His authority is the word of God, his religion is that of love, his inexhaustible theme is Christ. Such a work demands the highest development of all his physical and mental powers, and an unswerving consecration of heart and soul to the cause of his Master.

REFERENCES

1. Phillips Brooks, *Yale Lectures on Preaching.*
2. The *Secret of Effective Preaching,* delivered before the Free Church Congress, Cardiff, March, 1901. Hodder & Stoughton.
3. Quoted by Alexander Whyte, In Newman's *An Appreciation in. Two Lectures.*
4. *Representative Modern Preachers,* by Lewfs O. Brastow, D.D., Professor of Practical Theology in Yale University, The Macmllian Company, 1904.
5. *The Christian Ministry,* Lyman Abbott, quoted by Rev. Arthur S. Hoyt, in *The work of Preaching,* The Macmillan Company, 1905.

2 How to Develop Physical Power

It is as important for the public speaker to develop his body as to develop his mind. As the medium of expression it should be kept at the highest attainable point. Many of our most gifted speakers, especially clergymen, break down from lack of physical vigor, often just at the timc when their best work should be done. A strong mind in a strong body should be the aim of every public man.

Joseph Parker gave as his prescription for what he called "a great effort" in preaching a Turkish bath twice a week for three weeks, exercise on the hills every morning at daylight, a plunge in the sea in summer, and a vigorous run on the beach. "Then," said he, "there will be freshness in your breath, a ringing tone in your voice, and a substance in your muscle not soon exhausted. You will not enter the pulpit as a clammy, flabby old man with a heckling voice and a wandering eye, but as a giant ready for a giant's task."

A man should give a reasonable amount of time daily to his physical development. He should put to himself each night a series of questions to test his faithfulness in this respect. He may ask: Have I exercised my body sufficiently this day? Have I chosen the most nourishing food? Have I breathed deeply and abundantly of fresh air? Have I spent any time in the, sun? Have I given proper attention to bathing? Have I rested and relaxed at proper intervals? Have I been unduly hurried or excited? Have I washed out my system with generous drafts of pure drinking water? It would be advisable to write down a list of such questions in a notebook and keep a record for at least a month.

Demosthenes, in order to strengthen his lungs, used to repeat as many verses as he could in succession, climbing a hill. Gladstone chopped down trees for physical pastime. Spurgeon interested himself in geology in order to spend as much time as possible in the open air. Henry Ward Beecher gave particular attention to physical training, diet, and relaxation. Webster owed much of his greatness as a speaker to his commanding physique.

"Freshness of feeling," says Dr. Kennard, "will be preserved by maintaining a *healthy appetite and digestion.* Dyspepsia and the worries that wait upon its leaden steps are terribly aging. Care for the hygienics and athletics of his entire nature will reward him openly. He must not only work faithfully, but play regularly; must not only gird with mighty tension, but relax and rest at frequent intervals and give himself abundant sleep. Even the all-enduring camel must have his burden unloosed at night, but many a preacher never lays aside his heavy pack; he carries his church burdens the whole twenty-four hours and the whole twelve months through, and is writing sermons and settling disputes and raising church debts in his dreams. Is it any wonder that his soul grows seedy, and that he becomes mentally round-shouldered and decrepit?"[1]

The first great requisite for the public speaker

physically is a well-developed chest. This may be rapidly brought about by deep breathing exercises in the open air, and by combined breathing and physical exercises at home. After expanding the lungs somewhat fully, the chest should be gently tapped with the palms of the hands. It is helpful to rub the chest vigorously with salt and water, finishing with a rough towel. Habitually carry the chest high and full without undue straining.

The abdominal and waist muscles should be developed in a similar way. In taking a full breath, endeavor to expand the entire circle of the waist, then in exhaling allow the same muscles to contract Inhale and exhale suddenly several times, while expanding and contracting the abdominal muscles.

During these exercises the breath may be taken through the mouth and nose, but in repose use the nose exclusively. Through diligent practise deep breathing should become an unconscious habit. Many of our most successful pulpit and platform speakers attribute their power of endurance to deep breathing and the proper use of the abdominal muscles.

The entire surface of the body should be washed at least once a day. No arbitrary rules can be laid down for every one. Whether the bath be cold or warm, tub or sponge, must be left to the discretion and convenience of the individual. In a general way, however, it may be said that the best time for a hot bath is at night, and for a cold bath in the morning. After the bath the body should be thoroughly dried with a towel, finishing off with a hand-rubbing. If this is followed with light gymnastics, it will prevent one from taking cold. In any event the circulation should be stimulated. Whenever possible the exercises that follow should be practised in the open air, or near an open window. It should be remembered that deep breathing is the very foundation of good health.

COMBINED DEEP BREATHING, RELAXATION AND PHYSICAL EXERCISES

The advantage of these exercises is that they combine three in one, giving the greatest possible results in the time expended. They should commend themselves particularly to the busy man.

1. **The arms.** Thoroughly relax the arms at the sides, and while inhaling deeply raise them slowly until the hands meet as high as possible above the head. Clasp the hands tightly, hold the breath, make the upper chest and arms tense or rigid, then after a few moments gently relax, dropping the arms to the sides while exhaling evenly, slowly, and deeply. When the arms are properly tensed they will tremble.

2. **The chest.** Stand erect, chest active, arms stretched out in front with palms together. Swing the arms suddenly to the back, at the same time deeply inhaling and rising on the toes. Each time gently relax. The movement should be rapid and animated. Keep in mind that you are developing your chest.

3. **The legs.** Inhale deeply, fold the arms across the chest, then raise the body up and down on the toes ten times without touching the heels to the floor. Hold the breath throughout the exercise and avoid jerkiness in the movements.

4. **The thighs.** Inhale deeply, fold the arms, and while balancing yourself on the balls of the feet

sink to a sitting position, up and down, six times. Inhale as you go down, exhale as you come up.

5. **The abdomen.** Lie flat on your back. Raise the heels from the floor and bring the knees back toward the chest while deeply inhaling. Then thrust the legs out suddenly without touching the floor. Repeat in moderation.

6. **The legs relaxed.** Stand behind a chair to support yourself. Swing the right leg back and forth several times thoroughly relaxed. Repeat with the left leg. Avoid unnecessary movements of the rest of the body.

7. **The upper chest.** Inhale deeply, fully expanding the chest, and while holding the breath raise the shoulders up and down six times. Exhale very slowly.

8. **The waist and abdomen.** Stand erect, hands over head, palms front. Without bending the knees bend forward from the waist until the tips of the fingers touch the floor, at the same time inhaling a full breath. As you resume your upright position gently exhale and relax. In the first part of this movement tense the muscles of the legs and abdomen.

9. **Stationary running.** Begin a stationary running movement, very slowly at first, throwing the heels well up at back. Inhale and exhale very evenly through the nose and at regular intervals. Gradually increase the rapidity of the movement.

10. **Walking on all fours.** Walk about the room on all fours, breathing quietly and evenly. This will develop many of the muscles of the body and is

particularly good for reducing superfluous flesh around the abdomen.

This exercise may be varied by raising the legs straight up above the head and allowing them to drop slowly down again. Also by raising the body to a sitting position and bending forward as far as possible towards the toes. Practise these exercises very deliberately while breathing naturally and deeply.

REFERENCE

1. *Psychic Power in Preaching,* J, Spencer Kennard, D.D.

3 How to Develop the Speaking Voice

A well-trained voice is an instrument of great power in a public speaker. As the principal medium through which the preacher reaches his people it is worthy of the highest cultivation. Few men are gifted by nature with voices equal to all ordinary requirements, and in most cases it is a matter of long, earnest and systematic practise. Every man who speaks in public should acquire the power to use his voice in continued effort without weariness. A well-equipped speaker will know how to make his voice reach the furthermost auditor without noticeable effort. He will learn to unconsciously vary his voice in infinite ways to suit his varied thought. He will, in short, through pains-taking practise, develop his voice and bring it under the control of his will so as to make it respond to any demand he makes upon it.

The first aim in voice culture should be to secure a pure j quality of tone. That is to say, every particle of breath that is given out Should be converted into voice. This quality of voice is more agreeable to listen to than any other, it carries a greater distance, and is less strain upon the speaker himself. Pure tone is the natural and appropriate expression of pure thought, and the harmonious adjustment of all the vocal parts. In the exercises that follow, the mouth should be well open, and the breath applied to the vocal organs at first gently and continuously. The larynx should be *steadied,* but all rigidity of the throat muscles must be avoided. There should not be the slightest waste of breath. The ear of the student should be bent upon his voice that he may become in time his own best critic. Practise very softly at first, and persistently aim to produce a free, flowing, pure stream of voice.

1. Smoothness of tone. Stand easily erect, with chin level, the arms dropt loosely at the sides. Inhale through the mouth as if yawning, deeply but moderately, throwing out the abdomen and the upper chest. Place the lips in the position of *ah* as in the word father, and commence a singing tone on this vowel, aiming at softness and smoothness. While the tone is in progress observe closely whether any breath is escaping unvocalized, and if so, endeavor to hold it back in the lungs or "reservoir." Remember that in order to acquire steadiness and smoothness of voice, you must learn to apply to the vocal cords *just the amount of breath required* for a given tone; no more, no less. While the tone is in progress the mind should be constantly at work in a persistent effort to improve the quality of the voice.

Carefully observe the following: Open the mouth wide enough to let the tone out freely and softly; groove the tongue to give the mouth more of a funnel shape; depress the root of the tongue and raise the soft palate to give increased space at the back of the throat; and aim throughout the practise to turn every particle of breath into clear pure tone. Altho the voice should be quite soft in this exercise, it should be full and deep; that is to say, it should seem to come from the depths of the chest and not from the throat. The larynx should be *steadied,* but there should be no rigidity of the vocal apparatus. Liberate the throat muscles by thoroughly relaxing all the parts, and let the voice flow from the mouth freely.

Concentrate the mind, from time to time, on the muscles of the abdomen, so that all strain and effort will be there. Do not forget to keep the tone soft, steady, smooth, and deep. Keep the mouth wide open without undue exaggeration. Adhere strictly to one pitch at a time, but take all the various pitches in turn. The voice grows through use. At first take those keys that sound to you the best, and work up and down from them by degrees. Avoid extremes of pitch until there has been considerable practise on the middle keys.

Having secured a reasonably pure tone, aim next to direct the voice toward the hard palate—the hard bony arch just above the upper teeth. Prom this part of the mouth cavity the voice gets much of its "ringing" quality. Learn to attack the tone as soon as the mouth is opened. This exercise if faithfully practised each day for a few minutes, as prescribed, will enable you to get control of your voice, to get it properly "placed," and finally to secure a pure quality of tone. Practise moderately, in warm fresh air. Occasionally stand before a looking-glass during the exercise to observe your mouth and throat. Five minutes' practise is ample at the beginning.

2. Freedom of tone. Inhale as before, fully and deeply, open the mouth wide as in *ah,* but before actually commencing the tone, fix in your mind the pure quality of voice you wish to produce and *hear it mentally.* Then let the voice flow forth freely and smoothly, without any effort at the throat, all strain concentrated at the abdominal muscles, using these to back your tone up and to steady it. Remember—and this can not be too often repeated—you are to sing *through* the throat and not from it, that the tone is to seem to come from the very depths of the body, and that all effort must be from the abdominal muscles.

Time the duration of this tone from day to day, and endeavor to increase it. After a little practise there should be no difficulty in holding it half a minute or more.

3. Economy of breath. Inhale deeply, exhale softly on *ah,* stopping the tone short every few seconds, holding it and mentally counting four, then continuing and stopping at like intervals. This is to be done on a single breath and with open mouth. Aim to make the attack and close each time sharp and clear, but without added force. Apply the breath, but do not push it. Be careful not to squeeze the tone. Practise on all the pitches in succession.

4. Projection of tone. Inhale deeply, and exhale on singing *oo* as in boot. The shape of the lips in producing this vowel has a tendency to help the tone forward. Care should be taken, however, not to unnecessarily purse or pinch the lips. The lips should protrude as in whistling, but with a suggestion of relaxation. During this exercise it will prove helpful to send the tone forward to some imaginary person or object.

5. Roundness of tone. Inhale Deeply, and exhale on singing *o* as in old. The shape of the lips and mouth cavity in producing this sound suggests its character of roundness. It is a particularly valuable exercise for developing vocal purity and fullness. It should be noted that the vowel o has a distinctively rich quality, and this should be encouraged throughout this exercise.

Again inhale fully and deeply, but this time keep

the chest high, and active during the singing of the vowel, making the entire movement from the abdomen.

6. Blending of tone. Inhale deeply, and exhale on singing *oo, o,* and *ah,* blending them into one continuous stream of voice. The transitions from one vowel to the other should be very gradual. In this exercise the tone will seem to go forward of its own accord, and the student should assist this tendency.

7. Shock of the glottis. This exercise is to be practised with care and very moderately at first. Strike the voice softly but clearly on the element *hup,* taking a breath between each stroke. Keep to one pitch at a time, without the slightest variation. After a few strokes have been made in bright, clear tone, change to other pitches until the entire scale has been covered. This is a valuable exercise for clarifying the voice. As in previous exercises, the breath must not be heard.

Repeat this exercise in the elements *he, ha, haw, hah, ho,* and *hoo.* Take one element at a time and master it before proceeding to the next. Practise very slowly at first, but as facility is gained the speed may be increased.

EXAMPLES FOR PRACTISE IN PURE TONE

The following extracts contain a large number of open liquid sounds, and will be found useful in securing pure quality of voice. They should be read aloud, standing, with special regard to this quality, while endeavoring to apply the results of the previous exercises. To distinguish pure quality of tone may at first be difficult, but the student should persevere until the ear is trained to discern the slightest waste of breath during voice production.

1. I wandered by the brookside,
   I wandered by the mill;
I could not hear the brook flow,
   The noisy wheel was still;
There was no burr of grasshopper,
   No chirp of any bird,
But the beating of my own heart
   Was all the sound I heard.

I sat beneath the elm-tree
   And watched the long, long shade,
And as it grew still longer
   I did not feel afraid;
For I listened for a footfall,
   I listened for a word,
But the beating of my own heart
   Was all the sound I heard.

He came not—no, he came not;
   The night came on alone;
The little stars set, one by one,
   Each on his golden throne;
The evening wind passed by my cheek,
   The leaves above were stirred,
But the beating of my own heart
   Was all the sound I heard.

Fast silent tears were flowing,
   When something stood behind;
A hand was on my shoulder:
   I knew its touch was kind.
It drew me nearer, nearer;
   We did not speak one word,
For the beating of our own hearts
   Was all the sound we heard.

"The Brookside." **Richard Monckton Milnes**

2. Blow, blow, Thou winter wind,
Thou art not so unkind
   As man's ingratitude;
Thy tooth is not so keen
Because thou art not seen,
   Although thy breath be rude.

Heigh-ho! sing heigh-ho! unto the green holly:
Most friendship is feigning, most loving mere folly:
Then, heigh-ho! the holly!
This life is most jolly.

Freeze, freeze, thou bitter sky,
Thou dost not bite so nigh
As benefits forgot:
Though thou the waters warp,
Thy sting is not so sharp
As friend remember'd not.
Heigh-ho! sing heigh-ho I unto the green holly:
Most friendship is feigning, most loving mere folly:
Then, heigh-ho! the holly!
This life is most jolly.

"As You Like It." **Shakespeare**

3. Our bugles sang truce, for the night-clouds had lower'd,
And the sentinel stars set their watch in the sky;
And thousands had sunk on the ground overpower'd,
The weary to sleep, and the wounded to die.

When reposing that night on my pallet of straw
By the wolf-scaring fagot that guarded the slain,
At the dead of the night a sweet Vision I saw;
And thrice ere the morning I dreamt it again.

Methought from the battle-field's dreadful array
Far, far, I had roam'd on a desolate track:
'Twas autumn—and sunshine arose on the way
To the home of my fathers, that welcomed me back.

I flew to the pleasant fields traversed so oft
In life's morning march, when my bosom was young,
I heard my own mountain-goats bleating aloft,
And knew the sweet strain that the corn-reapers sung.

Then pledged we the wine-cup, and fondly I swore
From my home and my weeping friends never to part;
My little one kiss'd me a thousand times o'er,
And my wife sobb'd aloud in her fullness of heart.

"Stay—stay with us!—rest!—thou art weary and worn!"
And fain was their war-broken soldier to stay;—
But sorrow return'd with the dawning of morn,
And the voice in my dreaming ear melted away.

"The Soldier's Dream." **Thomas Campbell**

4. Abou Ben Adhem (may his tribe increase!)
Awoke one night from a deep dream of peace.
And saw, within the twilight in the room,
Making it rich, like a lily in bloom,
An angel writing in a book of gold.
Exceeding peace had made Ben Adhem bold,
And to the presence in the room he said,—
"What writest thou?"—The vision raised its head,
And with a look made of all sweet accord,
Answer'd, "The names of those who love the Lord,"
"And is mine one?" said Abou. "Nay, not so,"
Replied the angel. Abou spoke more low,
But cheerily still; and said, "I pray thee, then,
Write me as one who loves his fellow men."

The angel wrote, and vanish'd. The next night
It came again with a great wakening light,
And show 'd the names whom love of God had blest,
And lo! Ben Adhem's name led all the rest!

"Abou Ben Adhem and the Angel." **Leigh Hunt**

5. Full many a glorious morning have I seen
Flatter the mountain-tops with sovereign eye,
Kissing with golden face the meadows green;
Gilding pale streams with heavenly alchemy,
Anon permit the basest clouds to ride
With ugly rack on his celestial face,
And from the forlorn world his visage bide,
Stealing unseen to west with this disgrace:
Even so my sun one early morn did shine
With all-triumphant splendor on my brow;
But, out, alack ! he was but one hour mine,
The region cloud hath mask'd him from me now.
Yet him for this my love no whit disdaineth;
Suns of the world may stain, when heaven's sun
staineth.

Why didst thou promise such a beauteous day,
And make me travel forth without my cloak,
To let base clouds o'ertake me in my way,
Hiding thy bravery in their rotten smoke?
'Tis not enough that through the cloud thou break,
To dry the rain on my storm-beaten face,
For no man well of such a salve can speak
That heals the wound and cures not the disgrace:
Nor can thy shame give physic to my grief;
Tho thou repent, yet I have still the loss:
The offender's sorrow lends but weak relief
To him that bears the strong offense's cross.
  Ah! but those tears are pearl, which thy love sheds,
  And they are rich and ransom all ill deeds.

No more be grieved at that which thou bast done:
Roses have thorns, and silver fountains mud;
Clouds and eclipses stain both moon and sun,
And loathsome canker lives in sweetest bud.
All men make faults, and even I in this,
Authorizing thy trespass with compare,
Myself corrupting, salving thy amiss,
Excusing thy sins more than thy sins are;

For to thy sensual fault I bring in sense—
Thy adverse party is thy advocate—
And 'gainst myself a lawful plea commence:
Such civil war is in my love and hate,
  That I an accessory needs must be
  To that sweet thief which sourly robs from me.

"Sonnets." **Shakespeare**

6. Let us pass directly into the soul's history, and catch from what transpires in its first indications the sign or promise of what it is to become. In its beginning it is a mere seed of possibility. All the infant faculties are folded up, at first, and scarcely a sign of power is visible in it. But a doom of growth is in it, and the hidden momentum of an endless power is driving it on. And a falling body will not gather momentum in its fall more naturally and certainly than it will gather force in the necessary struggle of its endless life now begun. We may think little of the increase; it is a

matter of course, and why should we take note of it? But if no increase or development appears, if the faculties all sleep as at the first, we take sad note of that and draw, how reluctantly, the conclusion that our child is an idiot, and not a proper man! And what a chasm is there between the idiot and the man! One a being unprogressive, a being who is not a power; the other a careering force, started on its way to eternity, a principle of might and majesty begun to be unfolded, and to be progressively unfolded forever. Intelligence, reason, conscience, observation, choice, memory, enthusiasm, all the fires of his inborn eternity are kindling to a glow, and, looking on him as a force immortal, just beginning to reveal the symptoms of what he shall be, we call him man. Only a few years ago he lay in his cradle, a barely breathing principle of life, but in that life were gathered up, as in a germ or seed, all these godlike powers that are now so conspicuous in the volume of his personal growth. In a sense, all that is in him now was in him then, as the power of an endless life, and still the sublime progression of his power is only begun. He conquers now the sea and its storms. He climbs the heavens and searches out the mysteries of the stars. He harnesses the lightning. He bids the rocks dissolve, and summons the secret atoms to give up, their names and laws. He subdues the face of the world, and compels the forces of the waters and the fires to he his servants. He makes laws, hurls empires down upon empires in the fields of war, speaks words that can not die, sings to distant realms and peoples across vast ages of time; in a word, he executes all that is included in history, showing his tremendous energy in almost everything that stirs the silence and changes the conditions of the world. Everything is transformed by him even up to the stars. Not all the winds, and storms, and earthquakes, and seas, and seasons of the world have done as much to revolutionize the world as he, the power of an endless life, has done since the day he came forth upon it, and received, as he is most truly declared to have done, dominion over it.

And yet we have, in the power thus developed, nothing more than a mere hint or initial sign of what is to be the real stature of his personality in the process of his everlasting development. We exist here only in the small, that God may have us in a state of flexibility, and bend or fashion us, at the best advantage, to the model of His own great life and character. And most of us, therefore, have scarcely a conception of the exceeding weight of glory to be comprehended in our existence. If we take, for example, the faculty of memory, how very obvious is it that as we pass eternally on we shall have more and more to remember, and finally shall have gathered in more into this great storehouse of the soul than is now contained in all the libraries of the world. And there is not one of our faculties that has not, in its volume, a similar power of expansion. Indeed, if it were not so, the memory would finally overflow and drown all our other faculties, and the spirits, instead of being powers, would virtually cease to be anything more than registers of the past.

But we are not obliged to take our conclusion by inference. We can see for ourselves that the associations of the mind, which are a great part of its riches, must be increasing in number and variety forever, stimulating thought by multiplying its suggestives, and beautifying thought by weaving into it the colours of sentiment, endlessly varied.

The imagination is gathering in its images and kindling its eternal fires in the same manner. Having passed through many trains of worlds, mixing with scenes, societies, orders of intelligence and powers of beatitude—just that which made the apostle in Patmos into a poet, by the visions of a single day—it is impossible that every soul should not finally become filled with a glorious and powerful imagery, and be waked to a wonderfully creative energy.

By the supposition it is another incident of this power of endless life, that, passing down the eternal galleries of fact and event, it must be forever having new cognitions and accumulating new premises. By its own contacts it will, at some future time, have touched even whole worlds and felt them through and made premises of all there is in them. It will know God by experiences correspondingly enlarged, and itself by a consciousness correspondently illuminated. Having gathered in, at last, such worlds of premise, it is difficult for us now to conceive the vigor into which a soul may come, or the volume it may exhibit, the wonderful depth and scope of its judgments, its rapidity and certainty and the vastness of its generalizations. It passes over more and more, and that necessarily, from the condition of a creature gathering up premises into the condition of God, creating out of premises; for if it is not actually set to the creation of worlds, its very thoughts will be a discoursing in world-problems and theories equally vast in their complications.

In the same manner, the executive energy of the will, the volume of the benevolent affections, and all the active powers, will be showing, more and more impressively, what it is to be a power of endless life. They that have been swift in doing God's will and fulfilling his mighty errands, will acquire a marvelous address and energy in the use of their powers. They that have taken worlds into their love will have a love correspondently capacious, whereupon also it will be seen that their will is settled in firmness, and raised in majesty, according to the vastness of impulse there is in the love behind it. They that have great thoughts, too, will be able to manage great causes, and they that are lubricated eternally in the joys that feed their activity, will never tire. What force, then, must be finally developed in what now appears to be the tenuous and fickle impulse, and the merely frictional activity of a human soul.

"The Power of on Endless Life." **Horace Bushnell**

FLEXIBILITY OF TONE

1. **Speaking vowels.** Recite aloud, in clear speaking tones, *e, a, aw, ah, o,* and *oo,* first with rising inflection, then falling inflection. Next combine the two, making a circumflex inflection. Apply the breath to the vocal cords in just the right quantity. The tone should be bright and smooth.
2. **Alternating high and low.** Repeat the last exercise, in alternate high and low pitches. Do not move the head. Avoid extremes of pitch at first.
3. **Alternating loud and soft.** Repeat the vowels as before, in alternate loud and soft voice. The loud tones should not bc too loud, and the soft tones should be free from breathiness. Keep the head and body still.
4. **Varied inflection.** On the elements *le, la, law, lah, lo, loo,* practise first on a rising, then a falling inflection. The length of the inflection should vary from short, very short, long, and very long. All the keys of the speaking voice should be used, from high to low, and from loud to soft.
5. **Counting.** In pure, clear-cut voice, count from one to ten in one breath. Repeat in various pitches and inflections. Then count to twenty in one breath, to thirty, and longer if possible, but all *in one breath.*

EXAMPLES FOR PRACTISE IN FLEXIBILITY

These are to be recited aloud with all possible variety in keeping with the thought. There is up and down in thought, as well as gentleness and force. To bring out these appropriate elements is the work of the student in rendering the following examples. First analyze the extract silently to get a general idea of its meaning. Mentally picture each thought as vividly as possible.

1. From early childhood, even as hath been said,
From his sixth year, he had been sent abroad
In summer to tend herds: such was his task
Thenceforward till the later day of youth.
Oh, then, what soul was his, when, on the tops
Of the high mountains, he beheld the sun
Rise up, and bathe the world in light! Ha look'd—
Ocean and earth, the solid frame of earth
And ocean's liquid mass, beneath him lay
In gladness and deep joy. The clouds were touched,
And in their silent faces did he read
Unutterable love. Sound needed none,
Nor any voice of joy; his spirit drank
The spectacle; sensation, soul, and form
All melted into him; they swallowed up
His animal being; in them did he live,
And by them did he live, they were his life.
In such access of mind, in such high hour
Of visitation from the living God,
Thought was not; in enjoyment it expired.
No thanks he breath'd, he proffer'd no request;
Rapt into still communion that transcends
The imperfect offices of prayer and praise,
His mind was a thanksgiving to the Power
That made him; it was blessedness and love!

"The Excursion." **William Wordsworth**

2. Soft heath this elevated spot supplied,
With resting-place of mossy stone; and there
We sate reclined, admiring quietly
The frame and general aspect of the scene;
And each not seldom eager to make known
His own discoveries; or to favorite points
Directing notice, merely from a wish
T' impart a joy, imperfect while unshared.

That rapturous moment ne'er shall I forget
When these particular interests were effaced
From every mind! Already had the sun,
Sinking with less than ordinary state,
Attained his western, bound; but rays of light—
Now suddenly diverging from the orb,
Retired behind the mountain tops or veiled
By the dense air—shot upward to the crown
Of the blue firmament—aloft—and wide;
And multitudes of little floating clouds,
Pierced through their thin ethereal mold, ere we,
Who saw, of change were conscious, had become
Vivid as fire—clouds separately poised,
Innumerable multitude of forms
Scattered through half the circle of the sky;
And giving back, and shedding each on each,
With prodigal communion, the bright hues
Which from the unapparent fount of glory
They had imbibed, and ceased not to receive.
That which the heavens displayed, the liquid deep
Repeated; but with unity sublime!

While from the grassy mountain's open side
We gazed, in silence hushed, with eyes intent
On the refulgent spectacle, diffused
Through earth, sky, water, and all visible space,
The Priest, in holy transport, thus exclaim 'd:—
"Eternal Spirit! Universal God!
Power inaccessible to human thought
Save by degrees and steps which Thou hast deign'd:-
To furnish; for this image of Thyself,
To the infirmity of mortal sense
Vouchsafed; this local, transitory type
Of Thy paternal splendors, and the pomp
Of those who fill Thy courts in highest heaven,
The radiant cherubim;—accept the thanks
Which we, Thy humble creatures, here convened,
Presume to offer; we, who from the breast
Of the frail earth, permitted to behold
The faint reflections only of Thy face,
Are yet exalted, and in soul adore!
Such as they are who in Thy presence stand,

Unsullied, incorruptible, and drink
Imperishable majesty stream'd forth
From Thy empyreal throne, the elect of earth
Shall be—divested at the appointed hour
Of all dishonor—cleansed from mortal stain.
Accomplish, then, their number; and conclude
Time's weary course! Or, if, by Thy decree,
The consummation that will come by stealth
Be yet far distant, let Thy Word prevail,
Oh! let Thy Word prevail, to take away
The sting of human nature. Spread the law,
As it is written in Thy holy book,
Throughout all lands; let every nation hear
The high behest, and every heart obey!"

"The Excursion." **William Wordsworth**

3. For mark well, even in the course of a single night, changes may take place in human things without your being consulted which entirely alter your position; and each one who, instead of concerning himself with the common good, and regarding himself as a part of the great whole, has limited his interest to some narrow circle, perhaps opposed to the private interest of some one else; every one has a soul which, with all its desires and joys, its treasures and possessions, may in a night be required of him! And the more keenly the strife has been carried on, the less sure can human wisdom be of any firm ground or of any certain issue; the more foolish would it be to undertake to answer the question, Whose shall those things be which thou hast provided, or hast wished to provide? But where instead of strife and wrangling, instead of self-seeking and covetousness, that rule of life and feeling guides men which makes them rich in God; in that God who makes His sun shine on the evil and on the good, and sends rain on the just and on the unjust; in that God before whom all are equal, His fatherly love going forth to all; whose wise decrees are indeed hidden from us, so that we can never for one short moment lift the veil that conceals them, but whose laws and will are clearly revealed and should be written on the hearts of those

who confess the name of His Son;—among such people there is an end of this folly; each of them is willing that his soul should be called away at any moment; and such men know whose the things shall be which they have provided.

"True Harvest Joy." **F.E. Schleiermacher**

4. Have you ever seen a poor girl at midnight sitting down on a doorstep crying? Somebody passes by, and says, "Why do you sit here?" "I have no house, sir. I have no home." "Where is your father?" "My father's dead, sir." "Where is your mother?" "I have no mother, sir." "Have you no friends?" "No friends at all." "Have you no house?" "No; I have none. I am houseless." And she shivers in the chill air, and gathers her poor ragged shawl around her, and cries again, "I have no house—I have no home." Would you not pity her? Would you blame her for her tears? Ah! there are some of you that have houseless souls here this morning. It is something to have a houseless body; but to think of a houseless soul! Methinks I see you in eternity sitting on the doorstep of heaven. An angel says, "What! have you no house to live in?" "No house," says the poor soul. "Have you no father?" "No; God is not my Father, and there is none beside Him." "Have you no mother?" "No, the Church is not my mother; I never sought her ways, nor loved Jesus. I have neither father nor mother." "Have you no house, then?" "No; I am a houseless soul."

"Spurgeon'a Illustrative Anecdotes." **Louis Albert Banks**

5. Once more unto the breach, dear friends, once more;
Or close the wall up with our English dead!
In peace, there's nothing so becomes a man,
As modest stillness and humility:
But when the blast of war blows in our ears,
Then imitate the action of the tiger;
Stiffen the sinews, summon up the blood,
Disguise fair nature with hard favor'd rage,
Then lend the eye a terrible aspect;
Let it pry through the portage of the head,
Like the brass cannon; let the brow o'erwhelm it,

As fearfully as doth a galled rock
O 'erhang and jutty his confounded [1] base
Swill'd[2] with the wild and wasteful ocean.
Now set the teeth, and stretch the nostril wide;
Hold hard the breath, and bend up every spirit
To his full height.—On, on, you noblest English!
Whose blood is fet from fathers of war-proof,
Fathers that, like so many Alexanders,
Have, in these parts, from morn till even fought,
And sheathed their swords for lack of argument.
Dishonor not your mothers: now attest,
That those whom you called fathers did beget you:
Be copy now to men of grosser blood,
And teach them how to war! And you, good yeomen,
Whose limbs were made in England, show us here
The mettle of your pasture; let us swear
That you are worth your breeding, which I doubt not;
For there is none of you so mean and base,
That hath not noble luster in your eyes.
I see you stand like greyhounds in the slips,
Straining upon the start. The game's afoot;
Follow your spirit: and, upon this charge,
Cry—God for Harry! England! and Saint George!

"Henry V. to His Troops." **Shakespear**

6. In this refulgent summer, it has been a luxury to draw the breath of life. The grass grows, the buds burst, the meadow is spotted with fire and gold in the tint of flowers. The air is full of birds, and sweet with the breath of the pine, the balm of Gilead, and the new hay. Night brings no gloom to the heart with its welcome shade. Through the transparent darkness the stars pour their almost spiritual rays. Man under them seems a young child, and his huge globe a toy. The cool night bathes the world as with a river, and prepares his eyes again for the crimson dawn. The mystery of nature was never displayed more happily. The corn and the wine have been freely dealt to all creatures, and the never-broken silence with which the old bounty goes forward has not yielded yet one word of explanation. One is constrained to respect the perfection of this world in which our senses converse.

How wide; how rich; what invitation from every property it gives to every faculty of man! In its fruitful soils; in its navigable sea; in its mountains of metal and stone; in its forests of all woods; in its animals; in its chemical ingredients; in the powers and path of light, heat, attraction, and life, it is well worth the pith and heart of great men to subdue and enjoy it. The planters, the mechanics, the inventors, the astronomers, the builders of cities, and the captains history delights to honor.

But when the mind opens and reveals the laws which traverse the universe and make things what they are, then shrinks the great world at once into a mere illustration and fable of this mind. What am I? and What is? asks the human spirit with a curiosity new-kindled, but never to be quenched. Behold these outrunning laws, which our imperfect apprehension can see tend this way and that, but not come to full circle. Behold these infinite relations, so like, so unlike; many, yet one. I would study, I would know, I would admire forever. These works of thought have been the entertainments of the human spirit in all ages.

A more secret, sweet, and overpowering beauty appears to man when his heart and mind open to the sentiment of virtue. Then he is instructed in what is above him. He learns that his being is without bound; that to the good, to the perfect, he is born, low as he now lies in evil and weakness. That which he venerates is still his own, tho he has not realized it yet. *He ought.* He knows the sense of that grand word, tho his analysis fails entirely to render account of it. When in innocency or when by intellectual preception he attains to say,—"I love the Right; Truth is beautiful within and without forevermore. Virtue, I am thine; save me; use me; thee will I serve, day and night, in great, in small, that I may be not virtuous, but virtue";—then is the end of the creation answered, and God is well pleased.

The sentiment of virtue is a reverence and delight

in the presence of certain divine laws. It perceives that this homely game of life we play, covers, under what seem foolish details, principles that astonish. The child amidst his baubles is learning the action of light, motion, gravity, muscular force; and in the game of human life, love, fear, justice, appetite, man, and God, interact. These laws refuse to be adequately stated. They will not be written out on paper, or spoken by the tongue. They elude our persevering thought; yet we read them hourly in each other's faces, in each other's actions, in our own remorse. The moral traits which are all globed into every virtuous act and thought—in speech we must sever, and describe or suggest by painful enumeration of many particulars. Yet, as this sentiment is the essence of all religion, let me guide your eye to the precise objects of the sentiment, by an enumeration of some of those classes of facts in which this element is conspicuous.

The intuition of the moral sentiment is an insight of the perfection of the laws of the soul. These laws execute themselves. They are out of time, out of space, and not subject to circumstance. Thus in the soul of man there is a justice whose retributions are instant and entire. He who does a good deed is instantly ennobled. He who does a mean deed is by the action itself contracted. He who puts off impurity, thereby puts on purity. If a man is at heart just, then in so far is he God; the safety of God, the immortality of God, the majesty of God, do enter into that man with justice. If a man dissemble, deceive, he deceives himself, and goes out of acquaintance with his own being. A man in the view of absolute goodness, adores, with total humility. Every step so downward, is a step upward. The man who renounces himself, comes to himself. See how this rapid intrinsic energy worketh everywhere, righting wrongs, correcting appearances, and bringing up facts to a harmony with thoughts. Its operation in life, though slow to the senses, is at last as sure as in the soul. By it a man is made the Providence to himself, dispensing good to his good-ness, and evil to his sin. Character is always known. Thefts never enrich; alms never impoverish; murder will speak out of stone walls. The least admixture of a lie—for example, the taint of vanity, the least attempt to make a good impression, a favorable appearance—will instantly vitiate the effect. But speak the truth, and all nature and all spirits help you with unexpected furtherance. Speak the truth, and all things alive or brute are vouchers, and the very roots of the grass under-ground there do seem to stir and move to bear you witness. See again the perfection of the Law as it applies itself to the affections, and becomes the law of society. As we are, so we associate. The good, by affinity, seek the good; the vile, by affinity, the vile.

These facts have always suggested to man the sublime creed that the world is not the product of manifold power, but of one will, of one mind; and that one mind is everywhere active, in each ray of the star, in each wavelet of the pool; and whatever opposes that will is everywhere balked and baffled, because things are made so, and not otherwise. Good is positive. Evil is merely privative, not absolute: it is like cold, which is the privation of heat. All evil is so much death or nonentity. Benevolence is absolute and real. So much benevolence as a man hath, so much life hath he. For all things proceed out of this same spirit, which is differently named love, justice, temperance, in its different applications, just as the ocean receives different names on the several shores which it washes. All things proceed out of the same spirit, and all things conspire with it. Whilst a man seeks good ends, he is strong by the whole strength of nature. In so far as he roves from these ends, he bereaves himself of power, of auxiliaries; his being shrinks out of all remote channels, he becomes less and less, a mote, a point, until absolute badness is absolute death.

The perception of this law of laws awakens in the mind a sentiment which we call the religious sentiment, and which makes our highest happiness.

Wonderful is its power to charm and to command. It is a mountain air. It is the embalmer of the world. It is myrrh and storax, and chlorin and rose-mary. It makes the sky and the hills sublime, and the silent song of the stars is it. By it is the universe made safe and habitable, not by science or power. Thought may work cold and intransitive in things, and find no end or unity; but the dawn of the sentiment of virtue on the heart gives and is the assurance that Law is sovereign over all natures; and the worlds, time, space, eternity, do seem to break out into joy.

This sentiment is divine and deifying. It is the beatitude of man. It makes him illimitable. Through it, the soul first knows itself. It corrects the capital mistake of the infant man, who seeks to be great by following the great, and hopes to derive advantages *from another,* by showing the fountain of all good to be in himself, and that he, equally with every man, is an inlet into the steps of Reason. When he says, "I thought"; when love warms him; when he chooses, warned on high, the good and great deed; then, deep melodies wander through his soul from Supreme Wisdom. Then he can worship, and he enlarged by his worship; for he can never go behind this sentiment. In the sublimest flights of the soul, rectitude is never surmounted, love is never outgrown.

"The Divinity School Address." **Ralph Waldo Emerson**

ROUNDNESS AND RESONANCE OF TONE

The orotund voice is the simple pure tone rounded out into greater fullness. The word comes from *rotundus,* meaning round. It is produced mainly by an increased resonance of the chest arid mouth cavities, and a more vigorous action of the abdominal muscles. It always has the character of fullness, but is not necessarily a loud tone. Neither is it an "assumed" voice, but should result from expanded thought and increased intensity of feeling. Its force varies in degree with the thought being exprest It may be effusive or flowing, expulsive or rushing, explosive or bursting.

It is used in language of great dignity and power, in intense and ponderous thought, and in grandeur and sublimity. It is also used in public prayer, and in certain Bible and hymn reading. Coupled with the simple conversational style of speaking, it greatly enlarges the public speaker's possibilities of expression. It gives variety and appropriateness to the spoken word. An ordinary colloquial style of speaking, when long continued, becomes tame and uninteresting to an audience; but when all the gradations of soft, medium, and full orotund voice are added, the speaker is conscious of vastly increased scope and power.

It will be found helpful in the following exercises to keep the chest high and active throughout. The abdomen may expand and contract fully without letting the chest down from its full active position. If the student will also *think* depth and roundness during the exercises, it will assist in securing the desired qualities.

A resonant voice avails itself of all the various parts of the throat and chest that can contribute vibration. Like the strings of a violin or the stem of a tuning-fork, the voice needs some kind of solid body to give it character. This is imparted principally by the resonance chambers; *viz.*, by the cavities of the mouth and throat, by the chest, and by the facial resonators.

1. **Facial resonance.** The face immediately, surrounding the mouth and extending into the cheek bones can be employed to advantage in producing resonance. Inhale a full deep breath,

and begin a low *humming* sound on the element *maw*. Project the lips but do not part them, as the element is to be thought rather than exprest. The trembling sensation felt at the lips in producing this sound should be helped as much as possible until it extends up the face. This vibratory effect will be made to spread the more rapidly if the student thinks of circles while practising, of water rising from a fountain, or some other suggestive thought. While the humming is in progress keep to one tone at a time, but in turn change to other pitches. Aim to increase the vibrations and use considerable force in doing so. No harm can possibly come to the throat or voice through this exercise, so it may be practised with impunity.

2. **Open resonance.** Repeat the last exercise, but gradually open the mouth so that the element *maw* will pour forth in free liquid quality. There will be a tendency to lose the facial resonance as the mouth is opened, but this must be resisted. Open the mouth very gradually and endeavor to maintain the same degree of resonance throughout.

3. **Throat resonance.** Gently sing the vowel *e*, endeavoring to bring into vibration all the parts around the back of the mouth, particularly the soft palate and root of the tongue. As this vowel has a natural tendency to be throaty, great care should be taken to avoid rigidity and squeezing the tone.

4. **Chest resonance.** Inhale a full deep breath, and while singing the vowel *o* hold the chest high and rigid throughout the exercise. Think of the chest

as a sounding-board and make it vibrate as much as possible. Repeat this vowel in the speaking voice, with rising and falling inflection, following the directions given for the singing tone. As the tone is in progress think of roundness and fullness of voice. Hold in mind some lofty thought, or think of immensity, power, and majesty.

EXAMPLES FOR PRACTISE IN RESONANCE

1. My Lords, I do not mean to go further than just to remind I your Lordships of this,—that Mr. Hastings' government was one whole system of oppression, of robbery of individuals, of spoliation of the public, and of supersession of the whole system of the English government, in order to vest in the worst of all the natives all the power that could possibly exist in any government; in order to defeat the ends which all governments ought, in common, to have in view. In the name of the Commons of England, I charge all this villainy upon Warren Hastings, in this last moment of my application to you. Therefore, it is with confidence that, ordered by the Commons of Great Britain, I impeach Warren Hastings of high crimes and misdemeanors.

   I impeach him in the name of the Commons of Great Britain in Parliament assembled, whose parliamentary trust he has betrayed.

   I impeach him in the name of the Commons of Great Britain, whose national character he has dishonored.

   I impeach him in the name of the people of India, whose laws, rights, and liberties he has subverted, whose property he has destroyed, whose country he has laid waste and desolate.

   I impeach him in the name and by virtue of those eternal laws of justice which he has violated.

I impeach him in the name of human nature itself, which he has cruelly outraged, injured, and opprest, in both sexes, in every age, rank, situation, and condition in life.

"The Impeachment of Warren Hastings." **Edmund Burke**

2. Upon the principle on which the attorney-general prays sentence upon my client—God have mercy upon us! Instead of standing before Him in judgment with the hopes and consolations of Christians, we must call upon the mountains to cover us; for which of us can present, for omniscient examination, a pure, unspotted, and faultless course? But I humbly expect that the benevolent Author of our being will judge us as I have been pointing out for your example. Holding up the great volume of our lives in His hands, and regarding the general scope of them—if He discovers benevolence, charity and good will to man beating in the heart, where He alone can look; if He finds that our conduct, tho often forced out of the path by our infirmities, has been in general well-directed, His all-searching eye will assuredly never pursue us into those little corners of our lives, much less will His justice select them for punishment without the general context of our existence, by which faults may be sometimes found to have grown out of virtues, and very many of our heaviest offenses to have been grafted by human imperfection upon the best and kindest of our affections. No, gentlemen, believe me, this is not the course of divine justice, or there is no truth in the gospels of heaven. If the general tenor of a man's conduct be such as I have represented it, he may walk through the shadow of death, with, all his faults about him, with as much cheerfulness as in the common paths of life; because he knows that, instead of a stern accuser to expose before the Author of his nature those frail passages which, like the scored matter in the book before you, checker the volume of the brightest and best-spent life, His mercy will obscure them from the eye of His purity, and our repentance will blot them out forever.

"The Freedom of the Press." **Lord Erskine**

3. When Freedom from her mountain height
Unfurled her standard to the air,
She tore the azure robe of night,
And set the stars of glory there;
She mingled with its gorgeous dyes
The milky baldric of the skies,
And striped its pure, celestial white
With streakings of the morning light;
Then from his mansion in the sun
She called her eagle-bearer down,
And gave into his mighty hand
The symbol of her chosen land.

Majestic monarch of the cloud!
Who rear 'st aloft thy regal form,
To hear the tempest-trumpings loud,
And see the lightning lances driven,
When strive the warriors of the storm,
And rolls the thunder-drum of heaven;
Child of the sun! to thee 'tis given
To guard the banner of the free,
To hover in the sulfur smoke,
To ward away the battle-stroke,
And bid its blendings shine afar,
Like rainbows on the cloud of war,
The harbingers of victory!

Flag of the brave! thy folds shall fly,
The sign of hope and triumph high,
When speaks the signal trumpet tone,
And the long line comes gleaming on;
Ere yet the life-blood, warm and wet,
Has dimmed the glistening bayonet,
Each soldier eye shall brightly turn
To where thy sky-born glories burn,
And, as his springing steps advance,
Catch war and vengeance from the glance
And when the cannon-mouthings loud
Heave in wild wreaths the battle-shroud,
And gory sabers rise and fall,
Like shoots of flame on midnight's pall;
Then shall thy meteor-glances glow,
And cowering foes shall sink beneath

Each gallant arm that strikes below
  That lovely messenger of death.

Flag of the seas! on ocean wave
Thy stars shall glitter o'er the brave;
When death, careering on the gale,
Sweeps darkly round the bellied sail,
And freighted waves rush wildly back
Before the broadside's reeling rack,
Each dying wanderer of the sea
Shall look at once to heaven and thee,
And smile to see thy splendors fly
In triumph o'er his closing eye.

Flag of the free heart's hope and home,
  By angel hands to valor given;
Thy stars have lit the welkin dome,
  And all thy hues were born in heaven.
For ever float that standard sheet!
  Where breathes the foe but falls before us,
With Freedom's soil beneath our feet,
  And Freedom's banner streaming o'er us?

The American Flag." **Joseph Rodman Drake**

BRILLIANCY OF TONE

1. **"Bell" exercise.** Inhale deeply and fully; compress the air against the closed lips until they burst open on the word *bell.* Immediately place the tongue against the roof of the mouth to utter the sound of *l,* and hold the sound as long as possible, allowing it to die away very gradually in force. Avoid breathiness and violence in the explosion. Remember that the motive power should come from the abdominal muscles, and on no account from the throat. Practise this exercise rather gently at first, but later it can be done with increased sharpness and force.

2. **"Bell" resonance.** This is similar to the last exercise, but an effort is made to increase the vibration of the voice while dwelling on the letter *l.* This can be done by making the voice tremble and by manipulating the tongue slightly. Aim also to bring the head resonance more particularly into play.

3. **"Bell" varied.** Repeat the first exercise in great variety. Take first the middle pitches of the voice, then the upper and lower keys. Practise considerably on the very low pitches, aiming at clearness. Strike the word *bell* several times in quick succession. Imitate the striking of a bell, by clear cut blows, by swells of the voice, and other effects as they suggest themselves.

EXAMPLES FOR PRACTISE IN BRILLIANCY

1. Hear the sledges with the bells—silver bells—
What a world of merriment their melody foretells!
How they tinkle, tinkle, tinkle, in the icy air of night!
While the stars that oversprinkle
All the heavens, seem to tinkle with a crystalline delight;
Keeping time, time, time, in a sort of Runic rhyme,
To the tintinnabulation that so musically wells
From the bells, bells, bells, bells, bells, bells, bells—
From the jingling and the tinkling of the bells.
Hear the mellow wedding-bells, golden bells!
What a world of happiness their harmony foretells!
Through the balmy air of night how they ring out their delight!
From the molten-golden notes, and all in tune,
What a liquid ditty floats
To the turtle-dove that listens, while she gloats on the moon!
Oh, from out the sounding cells,
What a gush of euphony voluminously wells!

How it swells! how it dwells
On the Future! how it tells of the rapture that impels
To the swinging and the ringing of the bells, bells,
bells—
Of the bells, bells, bells, bells, bells, bells, bells—
To the rhyming and the chiming of the bells!
Hear the loud alarum bells—brazen bells!
What a tale of terror, now, their turbulency tells!
In the startled ear of night
How they scream out their affright!
Too much horrified to speak,
They can only shriek, shriek, out of tune,
In a clamorous appealing to the mercy of the fire,
In a mad expostulation with the deaf and frantic fire
Leaping higher, higher, with a desperate desire,
And a resolute endeavor, now—now to sit or never,
By the side of the pale-faced moon. Oh, the bells, bells,
bells!
What a tale their terror tells of despair!
How they clang, and clash, and roar! What a horror
they outpour
On the bosom of the palpitating air!
Yet the air, it fully knows,
By the twanging and the clanging,
How the danger ebbs and flows; yet the ear distinctly
tells
In the jangling and the wrangling,
How the danger sinks and swells,
By the sinking or the swelling in the anger of the
bells—of the bells—
Of the bells, bells, bells, bells, bells, bells, bells—
In the clamor and the clangor of the bells!
Hear the tolling of the bells—iron bells!
What a world of solemn thought their monody compels!
In the silence of the night,
How we shiver with affright
At the melancholy menace of their tone!
For every sound that floats
From the rust within their throats is a groan.
And the people—ah, the people—
They that dwell up in the steeple, all alone,

And who tolling, tolling, tolling, in that muffled monotone,
Feel a glory in so rolling on the human heart a stone—
They are neither man nor woman—
They are neither brute nor human—they are Ghouls:
And their king it is who tolls;
And he rolls, rolls, rolls, rolls a peean from the bells!
And his merry bosom swells with the peean of the bells!
And he dances and he yells;
Keeping time, time, time, in a sort of Runic rhyme,
To the peean of the bells—of the bells:
Keeping time, time, time, in a sort of Runic rhyme,
To the throbbing of the bells—of the bells, bells, bells,
To the sobbing of the bells; keeping time, time, time,
As he knells, knells, knells, in a happy Runic rhyme,
To the rolling of the bells—of the bells, bells, bells—
To the tolling of the bells, bells, bells, bells—
Bells, bells, bells—
To the moaning and the groaning of the bells.

"The Bells." **Edgar Allan Poe**

2. Thus saying, from her side the fatal key,
Sad instrument of all our wo, she took;
And, toward the gate rolling her bestial train,
Forthwith the huge portcullis high up-drew,
Which, but herself, not all the Stygian powers
Could once have moved; then in the keyhole turns
The intricate wards, and every bolt and bar
Of massy iron or solid rock with ease
Unfastens. On a sudden open fly,
With impetuous recoil and jarring sound,
The infernal doors, and on their binges grate
Harsh thunder, that the lowest bottom shook.
Of Erebus. She opened; but to shut
Excelled her power; the gates wide open stood,
That with extended wings a bannered host,
Under spread ensigns marching, might pass through
With horse and chariots ranked in loose array;
So wide they stood, and like a furnace-mouth
Cast forth redounding smoke and ruddy flame.

"Discord." **John Milton**

3. The multitude of Angels, with a shout
Loud as from numbers without number, sweet
As from blest voices, uttering joy—Heaven rung
With jubilee, and loud hosannas filled
The eternal regions. Lowly reverent
Toward either throne they bow, and to the ground
With solemn adoration down they east
Their crowns, inwove with amaranth and gold—
Immortal amaranth, a flower which once
In Paradise, fast by the Tree of Life,
Began to bloom, but, soon for Man's offense,
To Heaven removed where first it grew, there grows
And flowers aloft, shading the Fount of Life,
And where the River of Bliss through midst of Heaven
Bolls o'er Elysian flowers her amber stream!
With these, that never fade, the Spirits elect
Bind their resplendent locks, inwreathed with beams.
Now in loose garlands thick thrown off, the bright
Pavement, that like a sea of jasper shone,
Impurpled with celestial roses smiled.
Then, crowned again, their golden harps they took—
Harps ever tuned, that glittering by their side
Like quivers hung; and with preamble sweet
Of charming symphony they introduce
Their sacred song, and waken raptures high:
No voice exempt, no voice but well could join
Melodious part; such concord is in Heaven.

"Concord." **John Milton**

4. From Harmony, from heavenly Harmony
This universal frame began:
When Nature underneath a heap
Of jarring atoms lay
And could hot heave her head,
The tuneful voice was heard from high,
Arise, ye more than dead!
Then cold and hot and moist and dry
In order to their stations leap,
And Music's power obey.
From Harmony, from heavenly Harmony
This universal frame began:
From Harmony to Harmony

Through all the compass of the notes it ran,
  The diapason closing full in Man.
What passion can not Music raise and quell?
    When Jubal struck the chorded shell
His listening brethren stood around,
  And, wondering, on their faces fell
  To worship that celestial sound.
Less than a God they thought there could not dwell
    Within the hollow of that shell
    That spoke so sweetly and so well.
What passion can not Music raise and quell?

  The trumpet's loud clangor
    Excites us to arms,
  With shrill notes of anger
    And mortal alarms.
  The double double double beat
  Of the thundering drum
  Cries "Hark! the foes come;
Charge, charge, 'tis too late to retreat!"

The soft complaining flute
  In dying notes discovers
  The woes of hopeless lovers,
Whose dirge is whisper'd by the warbling lute.

Sharp violins proclaim
  Their jealous pangs and desperation,
  Fury, frantic indignation,
  Depth of pains, and height of passion
For the fair disdainful dame.

But oh! what art can teach,
What human voice can reach
  The sacred organ's praise?
Notes inspiring holy love,
  Notes that wing their heavenly ways
To mend the choirs above.

Orpheus could lead the savage race,
And trees uprooted left their place
Sequacious of the lyre:
But bright Cecilia raised the wonder higher
  When to her organ vocal breath was given

An Angel heard, and straight appear'd—
  Mistaking Earth for Heaven!

As from the power of sacred lays
  The spheres began to move,
And sung the great Creator's praise
  To all the blest above;
So when the last and dreadful hour
This crumbling pageant shall devour,
The trumpet shall be heard on high,
The dead shall live, the living die,
And Music shall untune the sky.

"Song for Saint Cecilia's Day." **John Dryden**

5. Near yonder copse, whore once the garden smiled,
And still where many a garden flower grows wild.
There, where a few torn shrubs the place disclose,
The village preacher's modest mansion rose.
A man he was to all the country dear,
And passing rich with forty pounds a year;
Remote from towns he ran his godly race,
Nor e'er had changed, nor wished to change his place;
Unskilful he to fawn, or seek for power
By doctrines fashioned to the varying hour;
Far other aims his heart had learned to prize—
More beat to raise the wretched than to rise.
His house was known to all the vagrant train;
He chid their wanderings, but relieved their pain.
The long-remembered beggar was his guest,
Whose beard, descending, swept his aged breast;
The ruined spendthrift, now no longer proud,
Claimed kindred there, and bad his claims allowed;
The broken soldier, kindly bade to stay,
Sate by his fire, and talked the night away—
Wept o'er his wounds, or, tales of sorrow done,
Shouldered his crutch, and showed how fields were
  won.
Pleased with his guests, the good man learned to glow,
And quite forgot their vices in their wo;
Careless their merits or their faults to scan,
His pity gave, ere charity began.

Thus to relieve the wretched was his pride,
And e'en his failings leaned to virtue's side;
But in his duty, prompt at every call,
He watched and wept, he prayed and felt for all;
And, as a bird each fond endearment tries
To tempt its new-fledged offspring to the skies,
He tried each art, reproved each dull delay,
Allured to brighter worlds, and led the way.

Beside the bed where parting life was laid,
And sorrow, guilt, and pain, by turns dismoved,
The reverend champion stood. At his control
Despair and anguish fled the struggling soul;
Comfort came down the trembling wretch to raise,
And his last faltering accents whispered praise.

At church, with meek and unaffected grace,
His looks adorned the venerable place;
Truth from his lips prevailed with double sway,
And fools, who came to scoff, remained to pray.
The service past, around the pious man,
With ready zeal, each honest rustic ran;
E'en children followed, with endearing wile,
And plucked his gown, to share the good man's smile.

His ready smile a parent's warmth exprest;
Their welfare pleased him, and their cares distrest;
To them his heart, his love, his griefs were given—
But all his serious thoughts had rest in heaven.
As some tall cliff that lifts its awful form,
Swells from the vale, and midway leaves the storm,
Tho round its breast the rolling clouds are spread,
Eternal sunshine settles on its head.
And e'en the story ran that he could gauge.
In arguing, too, the parson owned his skill,
For, e'en tho vanquished, he could argue still;
While words of learned length and thundering sound
Amazed the gazing rustics ranged around;
And still they gazed, and still the wonder grew,
That one small head could carry all he knew.

Oliver Goldsmith

"The Village Preacher," in "The Deserted Village."

VOLUME OF TONE

Adequate volume of voice is necessary in order that the public speaker, when occasion demands, should be able to fulfill all requirements. A voice suited to conversation may be wholly unsatisfactory when used in a large hall. How many men, addressing an audience probably for the first time, have been startled and embarrassed by the thinness and strangeness of their own voice.

Proper development of volume of tone, together with a little experience in public speaking, should enable an average person to readily adapt his voice to any ordinary auditorium. His aim should be to be easily heard in all parts of a hall, without undue elevation of pitch or noticeable physical effort.

Volume of voice does not necessarily mean loudness but rather fullness of tone. Its character is that of depth, roundness, and adequateness. It suggests power in reserve. It therefore inspires confidence both in the speaker and the hearer. As the voice grows through use, volume is to be acquired by practising daily exercises such as are here suggested. In all such practise there should be physical earnestness if the best results are to be secured. Half-hearted, lackadaisical efforts in any pursuit accomplish little. The student should bring his will to bear upon his work. Enthusiasm in the practise of voice exercises will naturally communicate itself to the speaker's public efforts.

It was the custom of Henry Ward Beecher to exercise his voice daily in the open air, exploding it upon all the vowel sounds. As a result of this practise, extending over a period of three years, he developed a voice remarkable for its power arid flexibility.

The following combinations should be practised aloud, in clear-cut tone, with abrupt movement of the abdominal muscles:

Be	ba	baw	hah	ho	boo
De	da	daw	dah	do	doo
Fe	fa	faw	fah	fo	foo
Ge	ga	gaw	gah	go	goo
He	ha	haw	hah	ho	hoo
Le	la	law	lah	lo	loo
Me	ma	maw	mah	mo	moo
Pe	pa	paw	pah	po	poo
Re	ra	raw	rah	ro	roo
Se	sa	saw	sah	so	soo
Te	ta	taw	tah	to	too
Ve	va	vaw	vah	vo	voo
We	wa	waw	wah	wo	woo
Ble	bla	blaw	blah	blo	bloo
Bre	bra	braw	brah	bro	broo
Che	cha	chaw	chah	cho	choo
Dre	dra	draw	drah	dro	droo
Dwe	dwa	dwaw	dwah	dwo	dwoo
Fle	fla	flaw	flah	flo	floo
Fre	fra	fraw	frah	fro	froo
Gle	gla	glaw	glah	glo	gloo
Gre	gra	graw	grah	gro	groo
Kle	kla	klaw	klah	klo	kloo
Kre	kra	kraw	krah	kro	kroo
Ple	pla	plaw	plah	plo	ploo
Pre	pra	praw	prah	pro	proo
Sle	sla	slaw	slah	slo	sloo
Sme	sma	smaw	amah	smo	smoo
Spe	spa	apaw	spah	spo	spoo

Sqe	sqa	sqaw	sqah	sqo	sqoo
Ske	ska	skaw	skah	sko	skoo
She	sha	shaw	shah	sho	shoo
Ste	sta	staw	stah	sto	stoo
Swe	swa	swaw	swah	Swo	swoo
Tre	tra	traw	trah	tro	troo
The	tha	thaw	thah	tho	thoo
Twe	twa	twaw	twah	two	twoo
Whe	wha	whaw	whah	who	whoo

key of sounds: *e* as in heal; *a* in hail; *aw* in haul; *ah* in hot; *o* in hole ; *oo* in boot.

EXAMPLES FOR PRACTISE IN VOLUME

1. There is a pleasure in the pathless woods,
   There is a rapture on the lonely shore,
   There is society, where none intrudes,
   By the deep sea, and music in its roar.
   I love not man the less, but Nature more,
   From these our interviews, in which I steal
   From all I may be, or have been before,
   To mingle with the universe and feel
   What I can ne'er express, yet can not all conceal

   Roll on, thou deep and dark blue Ocean—roll!
   Ten thousand fleets sweep over thee in vain,
   Man marks the earth with ruin—his control
   Stops with the shore;—upon the watery plain
   The wrecks are all thy deed, nor doth remain
   A shadow of man's ravage, save his own,
   When for a moment, like a drop of rain,
   He sinks into thy depths with bubbling groan,
   Without a grave, unknelled, uncoffined, and
   unknown.

   The armaments which thunderstrike the walls
   Of rock-built cities, bidding nations quake,
   And monarchs tremble in their capitals;
   The oak leviathans, whose huge ribs make
   Their clay creator the vain title take

Of lord of thee, and arbiter of war—
  These are thy toys, and, as the snowy flake,
They melt into thy yeast of waves, which mar
Alike the Armada's pride, or spoils of Trafalgar.

Thy shores are empires, changed in all save thee—
  Assyria, Greece, Rome, Carthage,—what are they?
Thy waters wasted them while they were free,
  And many a tyrant since; their shores obey
  The stranger, slave, or savage; their decay
Has dried up realms to deserts:—not so thou,
  Unchangeable, save to thy wild waves' play—
Time writes no wrinkle on thine azure brow—
Such as creation's dawn beheld, thou rollest now.

Thou glorious mirror, where the Almighty's form
  Glasses itself in tempests; in all time,
Calm or convulsed—in breeze or gale or storm,
  Icing the pole, or in the torrid clime
  Dark heaving;—boundless, endless, and sublime—
The image of Eternity—the throne
  Of the Invisible; even from out thy slime
The monsters of the deep are made; each zone
Obeys thee: thou goest forth, dread, fathomless, alone.

And I have loved thee, Ocean! and my joy
  Of youthful sports was on thy breast to be
Borne, like thy bubbles, onward: from a boy
  I wantoned with thy breakers—they to me
  Were a delight; and if the freshening sea
Made them a terror,—'twas a pleasing fear;
  For I WAS, as it were, a child of thee,
And trusted to thy billows far and near,
And laid my hand upon thy mans—as I do here.

"Apostrophe to ike Ocean."—"Childe Harold." **Byron**

Lesson talk. This selection should be read throughout in round, full-toned voice. Avoid mere loudness. Here and there the voice should swell in keeping with the thought. Try to picture in the imagination just what you are describing. Fit your voice to the thought. The general rate should be deliberate, but the pausing should be frequent and varied. Do not necessarily pause at the end of a line. Carefully analyze the meaning of each phrase, and pause according to the thought, not according to the lines nor even the grammatical punctuation. Look up in your dictionary the pronunciation of every doubtful word. Are you sure of these: Nature, ne'er, blue, ruin, depths, leviathans, Armada, Trafalgar, Assyria, realms, azure, torrid, wantoned, terror?

2. Hast thou a charm to stay the morning-star
In his steep course? So long he seems to pause
On thy bald, awful head, O sovereign Blanc!
The Arve and Arveiron at thy base
Rave ceaselessly; but thou, most awful Form!
Risest from forth thy silent sea of pines,
How silently! Around thee and above
Deep is the air and dark, substantial, black,
An ebon mass: methinks thou piercest it,
As with a wedge! But when I look again,
It is thine own calm home, thy crystal shrine,
Thy habitation from eternity!

O dread and silent Mount! I gazed upon thee,
Till thou, still present to the bodily sense,
Didst vanish from my thought: entranced in prayer,
I worship'd the Invisible alone.

Yet, like some sweet beguiling melody,
So sweet, we know not we are listening to it,
Thou, the meanwhile, wast blending with my thought
Yea, with my life and life's own secret joy:
Till the dilating Soul, enrapt, transfused,
Into the mighty vision passing, there,
As in her natural form, swell'd vast to Heaven!

Awake, my soul! Not only passive praise
Thou owest! Not alone these swelling tears,
Mute thanks and secret ecstasy! Awake,
Voice of sweet song! Awake, my heart, awake!
Green vales and icy cliffs, all join my Hymn.

Thou first and chief, sole Sovereign of the Vale!
O struggling with the darkness all the night,

And visited all night by troops of stars,
Or when they climb the sky or when they sink:
Companion of the morning-star at dawn,
Thyself Earth's rosy star, and of the dawn
Co-herald: wake, o wake, and utter praise!
Who sank thy sunless pillars deep in Earth?
Who fill'd thy countenance with rosy light?
Who made thee parent of perpetual streams?

And you, ye five wild torrents fiercely glad!
Who call'd you forth from night and utter death,
From dark and icy caverns call'd you forth.
Down those precipitous, black, jagged rocks,
For ever shatter'd and the same for ever?
Who gave you your invulnerable life,
Tour strength, your speed, your fury, and your joy,
Unceasing thunder and eternal foam?
And who commanded (and the silence came)
Here let the billows stiffen, and have rest?

Ye Ice-falls! ye that from the mountain's brow
Adown enormous ravines slope amain—
Torrents, methinks, that heard a mighty voice,
And stopt at once amid their maddest plunge!
Motionless torrents! silent cataracts!
Who made you glorious as the gates of Heaven
Beneath the keen full moon? Who bade the sun
Clothe you with rainbows? Who, with living flowers
Of loveliest blue, spread garlands at your feet?—
God! let the torrents, like a shout of nations,
Answer! and let the ice-plains echo, God!
God! sing, ye meadow-streams, with gladsome voice!
Ye pine groves, with your soft and soul-like sounds!
And they, too, have a voice, yon piles of snow,
And in their perilous fall shall thunder, God!

Ye living flowers that skirt the eternal frost!
Ye wild goats sporting round the eagle's nest!
Ye eagles, playmates of the mountain-storm!
Ye lightnings, the dread arrows of the clouds!
Ye signs and wonders of the elements!
Utter forth God, and fill the hills with praise!

Thou, too, hoar Mount! with thy sky-pointing peaks,
Oft from whose feet the avalanche, unheard,
Shoots downward, glittering through the pure serene,
Into the depth of clouds that veil thy breast—
Thou, too, again, stupendous Mountain! thou
That as I raise my head, awhile bow'd low
In adoration, upward from thy base
Slow traveling with dim eyes suffused with tears,
Solemnly seemest, like a vapory cloud,
To rise before me—Rise, O ever rise!
Rise like a cloud of incense, from the Earth!
Thou kingly Spirit throned among the hills,
Thou dread ambassador from Earth to Heaven,
Great Hierarch! tell thou the silent sky,
And tell the stars, and tell yon rising sun,
Earth, with, her thousand voices, praises god.

"Hymn to Mount Blanc." **Samuel Taylor Coleridge**

Lesson talk. This selection demands great variety in expression—changes of pitch, force and inflection. It offers a particularly good exercise for breaking up monotony. Note the musical effect in many of the sound-combinations—as in "some sweet beguiling melody," "voice of sweet song," "soft and soul-like sounds," etc.—and try to bring this musical effect out in your voice. Not only picture the various thoughts, but try to *realize* them at the moment of expression. The rate is slow and measured, but animated in feeling. Be sure of the pronunciation of these: Sovereign, Arve, Arveiron, ebon, dilating, ecstasy, countenance, perpetual, precipitous, jagged, invulnerable, avalanche, stupendous, mountain, suffused, hierarch.

3. What patriotic purpose is to be accomplished by this expunging? Is it to appease the wrath, and to heal the wounded pride of the Chief Magistrate? If he really be the hero that his friends represent him, he must despise all mean condescension, all groveling sycophancy, all self-degradation and self-abasement. He would reject with scorn and contempt, as unworthy of his fame, your black scratches, and your baby lines

in the fair records of his country. Black lines! Black lines! Sir, I hope the secretary of the Senate will preserve the pen with which he may inscribe them, and present it to that Senator of the majority whom he may select, as a proud trophy, to be transmitted to his descendants. And hereafter, when we shall lose the forms of our free institutions—all that now remain to us—some future American monarch, in gratitude to those by whose means he has been enabled, upon the ruins of civil liberty, to erect a throne, and to commemorate especially this expunging resolution, may institute a new order of knighthood, and confer on it the appropriate name of The Knight of the Black Lines.

But why should I detain the Senate, or needlessly waste my breath in future exertions? The decree has gone forth. It is one of urgency, too. The deed is to be done—that foul deed, like the blood-stained hands of the guilty Macbeth, all ocean's waters will never wash out. Proceed, then, to the noble work which lies before you, and like other skilful executioners, do it quickly. And when you have perpetrated it, go home to the people, and tell them what glorious honors you have achieved for our common country. Tell them that you have extinguished one of the brightest and purest lights that ever burned at the altar of civil liberty. Tell them that you have silenced one of the noblest batteries that ever thundered in defense of the Constitution, and bravely spiked the cannon. Tell them that henceforth, no matter what daring or outrageous act any President may perform, you have forever hermetically scaled the mouth of the Senate. Tell them that he may fearlessly assume what power he pleases, snatch from its lawful custody the public purse, command a military detachment to enter the hall of the Capitol, overawe Congress, trample down the Constitution, and raze every bulwark of freedom; but that the Senate must stand mute, in silent submission, and not dare to raise its opposing voice; that it must wait until a House of Representatives, humbled and subdued like itself, and a majority of it composed of the partizans of the President, shall prefer articles of impeachment. Tell them, finally, that you have restored the glorious doctrine of passive obedience and non-resistance; and if the people do not pour out their indignation and imprecation, I have yet to learn the character of American freemen.

"The Expunging Resolution." **Henry Clay**

REFERENCES

1. *Confounded.*—Vexed or troubled.
2. *Swill'd.*—Used for *washed much.*

4 How to Build A Vocabulary

A large and varied vocabulary is indispensable to the public speaker. With ten thousand words at his command he should be able to express himself with greater precision and effectiveness than with half that number. To increase his stock of words the speaker must cultivate an intense interest in them. He should form the habit of closely scrutinizing their meaning. He must know their intrinsic value as well as their outward effect. A peremptory challenge should be given to every word he does not thoroughly understand and its meaning studied in the dictionary.

Thoughts and words are intimately related, one being merely the expression or symbol of the other. Some authorities maintain that all thought to be clearly defined in the mind must appear there in so many words. It is true that there are many persons who, while reading silently, must say over each word in the mind in order to thoroughly understand and enjoy what they are reading.

It is difficult to overestimate the power of words. With them we command, we supplicate, we defy, we convince, we condemn, we conciliate. There are many dangerous and deadly "masked words" which everybody uses without understanding them, words colored by a man's own fancy, but which in turn mislead and poison him like so many "unjust stewards." To this class belong words of equivocation, exaggeration and sarcasm. The public, speaker's business is to find out the human meanings in words. He will do well, therefore, to heed the advice of Ruskin when he says:

"I tell you earnestly and authoritatively (I *know* I am right in this) you must get into the habit of looking intently at words, assuring yourself of their meaning, syllable by syllable—nay, letter by letter. For tho it is only by reason of the apposition of letters in the function of signs to sounds that the study of books is called 'literature,' and that a man versed in it is called, by the consent of nations, a man of letters instead of a man of books or of words, you may yet connect with that accidental nomenclature this real fact, that you might read all the books in the British Museum (if you could live long enough) and remain an utterly 'illiterate', uneducated person; but that if you read ten pages of a good book, letter by letter—that is to say, with real accuracy—you are forevermore in some measure an educated person. The entire difference between education and non-education (as regards the merely intellectual part of it) consists in this accuracy."

The study of words, if properly pursued, will prove a fascinating and beneficial exercise. There is an intrinsic pleasure in using the word that precisely expresses one's meaning. Such power and facility gives added self-confidence. It is told of Webster that once while addressing an audience he had difficulty in finding just the word he wanted. He discarded one after another until five or six had been disposed of, when suddenly he found the word he had been so earnestly seeking, and as he gave expression to it the audience, who had mentally followed his anxious search, burst out into spontaneous applause.

The possibility and potency of words is described by James Martineau, himself a master of word-painting: "Power they certainly have. They are alive with sweetness, with terror, with pity. They have eyes to look at yon with strangeness or with response. They are even creative, and can wrap a world in darkness for us or flood it with light. But in all this they are not signs of the weakness of humanity; they are the very crown and blossom of its supreme strength; and the poet whom this faith possesses will, to the end of time, be master of the critic whom it deserts. The whole inner life of men molds the forms of language and is molded by them in turn; and as surely pines when they are rudely treated as the plant whose vessels you bruise or try to replace with artificial tubes. The grouping of thought, the musical scale of feeling., the shading and harmonies of colour in the spectrum of imagination, have all been building, as it were, the molecules of speech into their service; and if you heedlessly alter its dispositions, pulverize its crystals, fix its elastic media, and turn its transparent into opaque, you not only disturb expression, you dislodge the very things to be exprest. And in proportion as the idea or sentiment thus turned adrift is less of a mere personal characteristic, and has been gathering and shaping its elements from ages of various affection and experience, does it become less possible to replace it by any equivalents, or dispense with its function by any act of the will."

Preference should be given whenever possible to the

short, simple Anglo-Saxon word. The study is not to resolve itself into mere "word-hunting" and a desire to dress one's thoughts in sesquipedalian language. It should be remembered that a large and ponderous vocabulary may be a hindrance rather than a help to expression. Edmund Burke frequently discloses this fault in his laborious and excessive precision. A multiplicity of words may so darken the windows of thought as to completely obscure all intellectual light The charm of the Gettysburg address lies chiefly in its simplicity of language, the proper expression of simplicity of thought Lincoln very early in life formed the "dictionary habit," and to this may be attributed his remarkable skill in the use of words.

Note how the, short word is employed to advantage in the following:

Think not that strength lies in the big round word,
Or that the brief and plain must needs be weak.
To whom can this be true who once has heard
The cry for help, the tongue that all men speak,
When want, or wo, or fear is in the throat,
So that each word gasped out is like a shriek
Prest from the sore heart, or a strange wild note
Sung by some fay or fiend? There is a strength
Which dies if stretched too far or spun too fine,
Which has more height than breadth, more depth than length.
Let but this force of thought and speech be mine,
And he that will may take the sleek, fat phrase,
Which glows and bums not, tho it gleam and shine,—
Light, but no heat—a flash, but not a blaze!
Nor is it mere strength that the short word boasts;
It serves of more than fight or storm to tell,
The roar of waves that clash on rock-bound coasts,
The crash of tall trees when the wild winds swell,
The roar of guns, the groans of men that die
On blood-stained fields. It has a voice as well

For them that far off on their sick-beds lie;
For them that weep, for them that mourn the dead;
For them that laugh, and dance, and clap the hand;
To joy's quick step, as well as grief's slow tread,
The sweet, plain words we learned at first keep time,
And, tho the theme be sad, or gay, or grand,
With each, with all, these may be made to chime,
In thought, or speech, or song, in prose or rime.

Addison Alexander

In his practical study of words the student should be supplied with a good dictionary, a book of synonyms, and blank note-books. A small vest-pocket note-book is desirable for jotting down words at a moment's notice.

The following exercises should be carefully practised, and can be indefinitely extended:

1. Write down in a column in your note-book the list of words here under. Then from memory write after each word its meaning and as many synonyms as you can. Compare the result with your dictionary.

copious	peculation	permeate
splenetic	impervious	obsequious
promiscuous	obsolete	deleterious
predatory	opprobrium	effloresce
miscreant	extenuate	indigent
propinquity	emolument	redundant
insidious	travesty	vicarious
circumscribe	vagary	initiative
tautology	sapient	lugubrious

2. Write down twenty-five words just as they occur to your mind, aiming to select the word next nearest in meaning, thus:

Abstemious, temperate, simple, genuine, reliable, stanch, enduring, firm, resolute, persevering, constant, invariable, immutable, stable, undeviating, steady, anchored, fixt, permanent, established, habitual, customary, usual, frequent, common.

3. Write down from, memory a list of twenty-five words in contrast, thus:

Cold, hot, cool, excited, calm, storm, quiet, noisy, silent, talkative, reticent, frank, secretive, enlighten, conceal, disclose, mask, indicate, equivocate, straightforward, deception, fidelity, perversion, scrupulous, exaggeration.

4. Select an original subject and write down all the words you can call to mind bearing upon it. Then augment your list from your dictionary and book of synonyms. Write out your composition and compare your effort with the following:

Subject: "Our Honored Bead."

List of words:

Honors, fortitude, patriotic, patience, death, redeemed, garnered, memory, precious, martyred, heroes, love, pride, inspiration, invisible, gladness, tears, country, mourners, liberty, justice, cherish, fresh, inscribed, remembrance.

How bright are the honors which await those who, with sacred fortitude and patriotic patience, have endured all things that they might save their nation from division and from the power of corruption! The honored dead! They that die for a good cause are redeemed from death; their names are gathered and garnered; their memory is precious; each place grows proud for them who were born there. There is in every village, and in every neighborhood, a glowing pride in its martyred heroes; tablets preserve their names; pious love shall renew the inscriptions as time and the unfeeling elements efface them. And the national festivals shall give multitudes of precious names to the orator's lips. Children shall grow up under more sacred inspirations, whose elder brothers, dying nobly for their country, left a name that honored and inspired all who bore it.

Oh, tell me not that they are dead, that generous host, that army of invisible heroes! Are they dead that yet speak louder than we can speak, and a more universal language? Are they dead that yet act? Are they dead that yet move upon society and inspire the people with nobler motives and more heroic patriotism? Ye that mourn, let gladness mingle with your tears; he was your son, but now he is the nation's; he made your household bright, now his example inspires a thousand households; dear to his brothers and sisters, he is now brother to every generous youth in the land; before, be was narrowed, appropriated, shut up to you; now he is augmented, set free and given to all; before, he was yours, now he is ours; he has died to the family that he might live to the nation. Not one name shall be forgotten or neglected, and it shall by and by be confest of our modern heroes, as it is of an ancient hero, that be did more for his country by his death than by his whole life.

O mother of lost children! sit not in darkness, nor sorrow when a nation honors. O mourners of the early dead! they shall live again, and live forever; your Borrows are our gladness; the nation lives because you gave it men that loved it better than their lives. And when the nation shall sit in unsullied garments of liberty with justice upon her forehead, love in her eyes, and truth on her lips, she shall not forget those whose blood gave vital currents to her heart, and whose life given to her shall live with her life till time shall be no more. Every mountain and hill shall have its treasured name, every river shall keep some solemn title, every valley and every lake shall cherish its honored register, and, till the mountains are worn out and the rivers forget to flow, till the clouds are weary of replenishing springs and the springs forget to gush and the rills to sing, shall their names be kept fresh with reverent honors which are inscribed upon the book of national remembrance.

"Our Honored Dead" **Henry Ward Beecher**

5. Write a speech on the subject, "The Murderer's Secret," employing the following list of words:

Aged, man, sleep, assassin, window, noiseless, lonely, moon, room, sleeper, murderer, fatal, blow, death, secret,

God, guilty, detection, conscience, torment, evil, entangle, violence, confession, suicide.

Then compare your speech with this:

An aged man without an enemy in the world, in his own house, and in his own bed, is made the victim of butcherly murder for mere pay. A healthful old man to whom sleep was sweet, the first sound slumbers of the night held him in their soft but strong embrace. The assassin enters, through the window already prepared, into an unoccupied apartment. With noiseless foot he paces the lonely hall half-lighted by the moon, he winds up the ascent of the stairs, and reaches the door of the chamber. Of this he moves the lock by soft continued pressure till it turns on its hinges, and he enters and beholds his victim before him. The room is uncommonly open to the admission of light. The face of the innocent sleeper is turned from the murderer, and the beams of the moon, resting on the gray locks of his aged temple, show him where to strike. The fatal blow is given, and the victim passes, without a struggle or a motion, from the repose of sleep to the repose of death. It is accomplished. The deed is done. He retreats, retraces his steps to the window, passes out through it as he came in, and escapes. He has done the murder. No eye has seen him. No ear has heard him. The secret is his own, and it is safe!

Ah! gentlemen, that was a dreadful mistake. Such a secret can be safe nowhere. The whole creation of God has neither nook nor corner where the guilty can bestow it and say it is safe. Not to speak of that Eye which glances through all disguises and beholds everything as in the splendor of noon, Such secrets of guilt are never safe from detection even by men. True it is, generally speaking, that "murder will out." True it is that Providence hath so ordained and doth so govern things, that those who break the great law of Heaven by shedding man's blood seldom succeed in avoiding discovery. Especially in a case exciting so much attention as this, discovery must come, and will come, sooner or later. A thousand eyes turn at once to explore every man, every thing, every circumstance, connected with the time and place; a thousand ears catch, every whisper; a thousand excited minds intensely dwell on the scene, shedding all their light, and ready to kindle the slightest circumstance into a blaze of discovery.

Meantime, the guilty soul can not keep its own secret. It is false to itself, or, rather, it feels an irresistible impulse of conscience to be true to itself. It labors under its guilty possession, and knows not what to do with it. The human heart was not made for the residence of such an inhabitant. It finds itself preyed on by a torment which it dares not acknowledge to God nor man. A vulture is devouring it, and it can ask no sympathy or assistance either from heaven or earth. The secret which the murderer possesses soon comes to possess him, and, like the evil spirits of which we read, it overcomes him, and leads him whithersoever it will. He feels it beating at his heart, rising to his throat, and demanding disclosure. He thinks the whole world sees it in his face, reads it in his eyes, and almost hears its workings in the very silence of his thoughts. It has become his master. It betrays his, discretion, it breaks down his courage, it conquers his prudence. When suspicions from without begin to embarrass him, and the net of circumstances to entangle him, the fatal secret struggles with still greater violence to burst forth. . It must be confest, it will be confest; there is no refuge from confession but suicide, and suicide is confession.

"The Murderer's Secret." **Daniel Webster**

6. Write an essay on the subject "Family Government," using the following list of words:

Command, decision, consistency, firmness, law, enforce, penalties, inevitable, consequences, uniformity, respect, administration, justice, severity, leniency, contemptible, transgression, impunity, coercive, despotism, discipline, governed, slavery, free, self-control.

Compare your composition with this:

Whenever you *do* command, command with decision and consistency. If the case is one which really can not be otherwise dealt with, then issue your fiat, and, having issued it, never afterward swerve from it. Consider well beforehand what you are going to do, weigh all the consequences, think whether your firmness of purpose will be sufficient; and then, if you finally make the law, enforce it uniformly at whatever cost. Let your penalties be like the penalties inflicted by inanimate nature—inevitable. The hot cinder burns a child the first time he seizes it; it burns him the second time; it burns him the third time; it burns him every time; and he very soon learns not to touch the hot cinder. If you are equally consistent, if the consequences which you tell your child will follow certain acts follow with like uniformity, he will soon come to respect your laws as be does those of nature.

And this respect, once established, will prevent endless domestic evils. Of errors in education one of the worst is that of inconsistency. As in a community crimes multiply when there is no certain administration of justice, so in a family an immense increase of transgressions results from a hesitating or irregular infliction of penalties. A weak mother who perpetually threatens and rarely performs, who makes rules in haste and repents of them at leisure, who treats the same offense now with severity and now with leniency, according as the passing humor dictates, is laying up miseries both for herself and her children. She is making herself contemptible in their eyes; she is setting them an example of uncontrolled feelings; she is encouraging them to transgress by the prospect of probable immunity; she is entailing endless squabbles and accompanying damage to her own temper and the tempers of her little ones; she is reducing their minds to a moral chaos, which after-years of bitter experience will with difficulty bring into order.

Better even a barbarous form of domestic government carried out consistently than a humane one inconsistently carried out. Again we say, avoid coercive measures whenever it is possible to do so; but, when yon find despotism really necessary, be despotic in good earnest. Bear constantly in mind the truth that the aim of your discipline should be to produce a self-governing being, not to produce a being to be governed by others. Were your children fated to pass their lives as slaves, you could not too much accustom them to slavery during their childhood; but, as they arc by and by to be free men, with no one to control their daily conduct, you can not too much accustom them to self-control while they are still under your eye.

"Education." **Herbert Spencer**

7. Carefully note the following phrases. Make similar lists of your own, gathered from your reading and observation.

kingly virtues	laborious indolence
dazzling contrasts	violet valley
barren phraseology	panic terror
consummate prudence	impregnable stronghold
legendary valor	unreasoning felicity
teeming millions	noble zeal
triumphant victory	riotous vegetation
timid mediocrity	tacit assumption
bloated epicure	unwearied enthusiasm
unutterablc forces	throbbing personality
extreme rarity	utterly relentless
unmasked pretension	predestinated criminals
youthful buoyancy	pitiless persecution
luminous insight	sublime achievement
unfailing tact	fundamental principle
matured skill	immeasurable power
capacious understanding	unbending strength
lawless violence	twilight glimmerings
searching sunlight	kindled imagination
copious fountain	softening influences
sun-baked hills	glorious iconoclasts
implacable fervor	momentous crisis
enlightened judgment	trembling solicitude
touching fidelity	inviolable justice
abundant recognition	innocent stratagem

8. Note three special words each day in your reading or in the conversation of others, and employ them in your speech that day. Keep a record of such words for frequent review. If this practise is faithfully carried out your vocabulary will be surprizingly increased in a short time.

9. Write in your note-book, daily, at least seven words from the following lists, in the order given. Then after each word write a sentence illustrating its idiomatic use. Afterward compare with your dictionary.

WORD LIST

I. ABSTRACT RELATIONS

Essence, subjectiveness, pith, principle, quintessence, incarnation, soul.

Circumstance, phase, attitude, occasion, situation, juncture, place.

Contrary, opposed, antithetical, contrasted, conflicting, hostile, antipodean.

Agreement, accordance, unison, harmony, conformity, consonance, concord.

Equality, parity, balance, poise, evenness, symmetry, level.

Greatness, magnitude, immensity, enormity, infinity, largeness, might.

Vast, towering, stupendous, prodigious, astonishing, incredible, marvelous.

Supreme, paramount, preeminent, crowning, inimitable, superlative, incomparable.

Increase, exalt, strengthen, intensify, raise, augment, enlarge.

Disperse, scatter, dispel, apportion, sow, disseminate, spread.

Infinite, exhaustless, incomprehensible, perpetual, measureless, incalculable, boundless.

Continual, endless, interminable, unceasing, eternal, incessant, uninterrupted.

Previous, prior, preceding, antecedent, former, aforesaid, foregoing.

Venerable, superannuated, decrepit, antiquated, declining, patriarchal, waning.

Capricious, desultory, fitful, uncertain, whimsical, unsteady, spasmodic.

Variation, modification, change, alteration, permutation, qualification, deviation.

Fluctuate, waver, vacillate, oscillate, vary, flutter, scruple.

Power, strength, energy, force, virility, vitality, vigor.

Powerful, robust, potent, hardy, puissant, mighty, sturdy.

Calm, cool, tranquillize, assuage, appease, compose, palliate.

II. SPACE

Extent, expanse, scope, range, latitude, compass, field.

Diminish, compress, dwarf, circumscribe, contract, condense, lessen.

Proximity, nearness, propinquity, vicinity, adjacency, contiguity, neighborhood.

Abridge, curtail, shorten, reduce, abbreviate, prune, epitomize.

Height, eminence, elevation, altitude, loftiness, pitch, sublimity.

Encompass, surround, enclose, circumvent, gird, beset, encircle.

Rotund, round, cylindrical, spherical, bulbous, circular, complete.

Smooth, polished, slippery, velvety, lubricous, glabrous, glossy.

Velocity, swiftness, speed, expedition, celerity, rapidity, acceleration.

Gentle, easy, leisurely, imperceptible, gradual, deliberate, slow.

Discursive, devious, vagrant, circuitous, rambling, erratic, desultory.

Entrance, introgression, intrusion, incursive, invasion, admission, insinuation.

Expansion, enlargement, increase, augmentation, amplification, swell, inflation.

Emaciated, lean, gaunt, lanky, skinny, starved, meager.

Symmetry, shapeliness, finish, beauty, proportion, uniformity, regularity.

Involved, intricate, complicated, labyrinthine, winding, con-voluted, twisted.

Protuberance, swelling, projection, protrusion, bulge, convexity, prominence.

Pointed, conical, tapering, pyramidal, sharp, keen, acute.

Propel, throw, pitch, project, fling, cast, toss. Tremulous, shambling, convulsive, restless, agitated, shaking, unquiet.

III. MATTER

Subtile, weightless, ethereal, sublimated, volatile, buoyant, floating.

Congeal, coagulate, crystallize, petrify, solidify, consolidate, fix.

Flexible, supple, pliant, limber, plastic, tractable, malleable.

Powdery, granular, mealy, impalpable, efflorescent, sabulous, flocculent.

Ferment, effervesce, bubble, gurgle, foam, froth, boil.

Oily, unctuous, sebaceous, greasy, saponaceous, fatty, slippery.

Agreeable, refreshing, comforting, cordial, genial, palatable, sensuous.

Heat, caloric, fervor, warmth, incandescence, glow, hectic.

Pungent, strong, sharp, stinging, biting, acrimonious, peppery.

Fragrant, aromatic, spicy, balmy, scented, redolent, perfumed.

Inaudible, stifled, low, dull, muffled, hoarse, husky.

Scream, screech, shriek, yell, roar, shout, halloo.

Melodious, musical, tuneful, sweet, dulcet, mellifluous, euphonious.

Luminous, vivid, lucid, lambent, lustrous, scintillant, bright.

Turbid, muddy, obfuscated, cloudy, thick, fuliginous, muggy.

Behold, discern, perceive, descry, distinguish, recognize, see.

Visible, palpable, perceptible, discernible, apparent, obvious, plain.

Variegated, kaleidoscope, iridescent, opalescent, prismatic, diversified, tesselated.

Black, swarthy, sable, somber, dark, jetty, ebon.

Silence, stillness, peace, hush, lull, muteness, soundless.

IV. INTELLECT

Conception, thought, apprehension, perception, impression, idea, notion.

Alertness, vigilance, attention, prudence, forethought, precaution, watchfulness.

Discrimination, distinction, nicety, differentiation, distinguish-ing, estimation, discernment.

Reasonable, credible, probable, plansible, presumable, ostensible, likely.

Absolute, positive, definite, unequivocal, unmistakable, decisive, clear.

Sophistry, perversion, casuistry, equivocation, evasion, chicanery, speciousness.

Refute, disprove, invalidate, demolish, rebut, parry, expose.

Belief, credence, assurance, faith, confidence, dependence, credit.

Incredulous, supsicious, scrupulous, distrustful, skeptical, inconvincible, unbelieving.

Dissent, demur, differ, protest, repudiate, contradict, disagree.

Exact, definite, precise, literal, unerring, rigid, scrupulous.

Twaddle, jargon, moonshine, vagary, fustian, stuff, tomfoolery.

Acumen, subtlety, perspicacity, sagacity, acuteness, comprehension, intelligence.

Foolish, unwise, ridiculous, stupid, asinine, irrational, injudicious.

Madness, delirium, frenzy, lunacy, aberration, delusion, hallucination.

Portend, signify, augur, typify, presage, herald, foreshadow.

Conjecture, surmise, suspect, suppose, presume, divine, speculate.

Fabulous, legendary, chimerical, fantastical, imaginary, mythological, visionary.

Unreasonable, inconsistent, untenable, fallacious, groundless, illogical, invalid.

Ambiguous, equivocal, vague, indefinite, questionable, doubtful, dubious.

V. VOLITION

Persevering, unfaltering, industrious, persisting, unflinching, strenuous, unwavering.

Tergiversation, recantation, retraction, withdrawal, disavowal, renunciation, defection.

Attraction, allurement, enticement, cajolery, inducement, temptation, fascination.

Adequacy, abundance, copiousness, amplitude, profusion, luxuriance, plentitude.

Redundant, exuberant, inordinate, excessive, profuse, replete, extravagant.

Contemptible, meager, beggarly, miserable, shabby, wretched, paltry.

Inexpedient, objectionable, disadvantageous, inopportune, undesirable, inappropriate, ineligible.

Perfect, faultless, immaculate, spotless, impeccable, unblemished, complete.

Morbid, unsound, vitiated, contaminated, infirm, drooping, diseased.

Salubrious, wholesome, sanitary, invigorating, nutritious, hygienic, healthful.

Dulness, languor, sluggishness, drowsiness, lethargy, heaviness, torpidity.

Skill, adroitness, proficiency, facility, expertness, dexterity, mastery.

Ingenuous, unaffected, guileless, unsophisticated, artless, simple, docile.

Manageable, tractable, submissive, yielding, ductile, pliant, towardly.

Variance, disagreement, dissension, misunderstanding, division, disunion, breach.

Pacify, compose, reconcile, placate, conciliate, propitiate, harmonize.

Succumb, submit, yield, resign, bend, capitulate, surrender.

Accomplish, achieve, compass, consummate, perfect, complete, elaborate.

Defeat, conquer, silence, vanquish, discomfit, overcome, check-mate.

Prosperous, thriving, buoyant, fortunate, lucky, successful, affluent.

VI. AFFECTIONS

Insensible, apathetic, frigid, dull, phlegmatic, obtuse, cold.

Excitement, impetuosity, paroxysm, perturbation, vehemence, agitation, ferment.

Felicitous, delightful, charming, exquisite, lovely, winning, captivating.

Vivacity, animation, liveliness, jocundity, joviality, alacrity, life.

Lugubrious, funereal, somber, melancholy, gloomy, spiritless, mournful.

Lachrymose, melancholic, hypochondriacs, saturnine, splenetic, pensive, sad.

Facetiousness, waggery, smartness, whimsicality, banter, jocularity, humor.

Beautiful, handsome, lovely, elegant, comely, refined, dainty.

Pure, chaste, cultivated, refined, classical, esthetic, artistic.

Ridiculous, ludicrous, funny, laughable, grotesque, farcical, whimsical.

Confident, sanguine, buoyant, elated, enthusiastic, utopian, exultant.

Fear, diffidence, apprehension, misgiving, timidity, perturbation, trepidation.

Courage, bravery, valor, confidence, intrepidity, gallantry, daring.

Repugnance, disgust, loathing, antipathy, abhorrence, animosity, detestation.

Surprize, astonish, astound, amaze, bewilder, stagger, startle.

Illustrious, glorious, imperishable, brilliant, eminent, peerless, immortal.

Insolent, arrogant, imperious, haughty, dictatorial, arbitrary, supercilious.

Affectionate, sympathetic, loving, tender, ardent, rapturous, devoted.

Benevolence, unselfishness, philanthropy, benignity, kindness, charity, generosity.

Respect, courtesy, reverence, deference, veneration, esteem, regard.

5 Power in English Style

An element of great power and effectiveness in public speaking is a good English style. Among the many definitions of this phrase are these: Newman: "Style is a thinking out into language." Wordsworth: "Style is the incarnation of thought" Buffon: "Style is the man." Dean Swift: "Style is proper words in proper places." Pater: "Truth! there can be no merit, no craft at all, without that." Phelps: "Style is the general term by which we designate the qualities of thought as exprest in language." W. J. Dawson: "Greatness of style springs from the great mind and the noble temper."

Style, then, is the result of a certain moral and mental discipline, in which a man at last expresses *himself.* As a result of this training words will fit naturally and readily into their proper places, while their arrangement will suggest clearness, rhythm, beauty, force, felicity, and other qualities. Carlyle says: "Care not for the reward of your speaking, but simply and with undivided mind for the *truth* of your speaking." Jean Paul Richter's counsel to the writer is equally applicable to the speaker: "Never write upon a subject without having first *read* yourself full of it, and never read without having first *thought* yourself hungry."

According to leading rhetoricians, the principal

qualities to be developed are purity, precision, perspicuity, individuality, energy, elegance, and naturalness. To this end the writer and speaker will endeavor to make these a part of his general mental habits. As a man accustoms himself to think, so is he likely to speak, or "As a man thinketh, so is he." He should closely study such masters of prose style as Macaulay, Newman, Ruskin, Matthew Arnold, and others, reading them aloud, and committing them to writing.

A favourite model for students of English style is John Henry Newman, of whom Alexander Whyte says:

"The strength, the richness, the pliability, the acuteness, the subtlety, the spiritualness, the beauty, the manifold resources of the English language, are all brought out under Newman's hand, as under the hand of no other English author. 'Athanasius is a great writer,' says Newman, 'simple in his diction, clear, unstudied, direct, vigorous, elastic, and, above all, characteristic.' All of which I will repeat of Newman himself, and especially this—he is, above all, characteristic. If the English language has an angel residing in it and presiding over it, surely Newman is that angel. Or, at the least, the angel who has the guardianship of the English language committed to him must surely have handed his own pen to Newman as often as that master has sat down to write English. No other writer in the English language has ever written it quite like Newman. Every preface of his, every title-page of his, every dedication and advertisement of his, every footnote, every parenthesis of his, has a stamp upon it that at once makes you say—that is Newman! He is simply inimitable. He is simply alone as a writer, and has no fellow."

Contrast with this high tribute the eloquent words

of Newman himself: "While the many use language as they find it, the man of genius uses it indeed, but subjects it withal to his own purposes, and molds it according to his own peculiarities. The throng and succession of ideas, thoughts, feelings, imaginations, aspirations, which pass within him, the abstractions, the juxtapositions, the comparisons, the discriminations, the conceptions, which are so original in him, his views of external things, his judgments upon life, manners, and history, the exercises of his wit, of his humor, of his depth, of his sagacity, all these in-numerable and incessant creations, the very pulsation and throbbing of his intellect, does he image forth, to all does he give utterance, in a corresponding language, which is as multiform as this inward mental action itself and analogous to it, the faithful expression of his intense personality, attending on his own inward world of thought as its very shadow: so that we might as well say one man's shadow is another's as that the style of a really gifted mind can belong to any but himself. It follows him about as a shadow. His thought and feeling are personal, and so his language is personal."

According to Newman's definition, thought and speech are inseparable, so that a man who aspires to write well or to speak well should see to it that he first *thinks* well. Since the time of Cicero and Quintilian the advice given in this matter of English style has been to write, write, write. This applies to original writing as well as to copying the thoughts and language of others. This work should be done every day, and as much of it as possible. Macaulay wrote six pages every morning, reducing his first rough draft to two pages, and considered his day ill-spent when he neglected to do this. He was emphatic in his dislike for "fine writing," and said: "The feelings should, indeed, have their ornamental garb, but, like an elegant woman, they should be neither muffled nor exposed. The drapery should be so arranged as at once to answer the purposes of modest concealment and judicious display."

As a model of purity of style the Bible offers an incomparable text. In combining simplicity of expression and sublimity of thought what outside of its holy pages can equal this: "Let there be light: and there was light!" And yet according to the style of some speakers, this would be rendered, as William Matthews says: "Let there be light, and there was a solar illumination!" In all the noted lists of "One hundred best books" the Bible is given first place. Archbishop Fenelon says: "The Scripture surpasses the most ancient Greek authors vastly in native simplicity, loveliness, and grandeur. Homer himself never reached the sublimity of Moses' songs. Never did any ode, either Greek or Latin, come up to the loftiness of the Psalms. Neither Homer nor any other great poet equaled Isaiah, describing the majesty of God. What is there in antiquity that can be compared to the lamentations of Jeremiah, when he tenderly deplores the misery of his country, or the prophecy of Nahum, when he foresees in the spirit the proud Nineveh fall under the rage of an invisible army? Everything is painted in such a lively manner as strikes the imagination: the prophet far outdoes Homer. Read likewise Daniel denouncing to Belshazzar the divine vengeance ready to overwhelm him, and try if you can find anything in the most sublime original of antiquity that can be compared to those passages of Sacred Writ. As for the rest of Scripture, every portion of it is uniform and constant, every part bears the peculiar character that becomes it. In short, there is as much difference between the heathen poet and the prophets as there is between a false enthusiasm and the true."

Sympathy, simplicity, enthusiasm, vitality, power, loftiness of spirit, love of truth, and other such qualities in the public speaker should first characterize his thinking habits, that they may naturally reflect themselves in the personality of his English style. Daily practise in writing stimulates the mental faculties, promotes accuracy and precision, and tends to make one systematic and logical. The prudent writer or speaker will avoid all attempts at "flowers of rhetoric," "fine writing," and "perfumed fancy" as having a tendency to impoverish his natural expression.

The public speaker should write for the car as well as for the eye. He will summon his audience before him, gather the people around him in imagination, and mentally voice his thoughts to them as he writes. He should frequently stop writing and read aloud what he has written to determine whether it fits the mouth and "speaks well." Otherwise he may be composing a very good essay but a very poor speech. The ear is the most exacting critic in this matter. It is quick to detect a word out of place, an inharmonious combination of sounds, or other infelicity of speech.

The public speaker will have a scholarly care about his habits of conversation. He will not only avoid loose and in-correct speech, but will constantly aim to express himself at his best, without resorting to pedantry or stiltedness.

"We must write as carefully, and as much as we can," says Quintilian; "for as the ground, by being dug to a great depth, becomes more fitted for fructifying and nourishing seeds, so improvement of the mind, acquired from more than mere superficial cultivation, pours forth the fruits of study in richer abundance, and retains them with greater fidelity. For without this precaution, the very faculty of speaking extempore will but furnish us with empty loquacity, and words born on the lips. In writing are the roots, in writing are the foundations of eloquence; by writing resources are stored up, as it were, in a sacred repository, whence they may be drawn forth for sudden emergencies, or as circumstances require."[1]

The constant aim of the writer and speaker should be toward simplicity. He should prefer the short Saxon word, whenever possible, instead of the usually ponderous importation from some other language. Simplicity begets clearness, and clearness of thought and expression are the fundamental qualities for deeply impressing an audience. Particularly should the student guard against a style like the following:

"All external objects are in their truest sense visible embodiments or incarnations of divine ideas which are roughly sculptured in the hard granite that underlies the living and breathing surface of the world above; penciled in delicate tracery upon each bark-flake that encompasses the tree-trunk, each leaf that trembles in the breeze, each petal that fills the air with fragrant effluence; assuming a living and breathing existence in the rhythmic throbbings of the heart-pulse that urges the life-stream through the body of every animated being; and attaining their greatest perfection in man, who is thereby bound by the very fact of his existence to outspeak and outact the divine ideas which are the true instincts of humanity, before they are crusht or paralyzed by outward circumstances."

The student is not recommended to devote himself too exclusively to any one writer. It is better to give some time to each of the recognized stylists. For simplicity he will study the Bible, Bunyan, Addison, and Lincoln; for elegance and resourcefulness, John Henry Newman, Washington Irving, and James Martineau; for rhetorical style, Macaulay; for narrative and character delineation, Dickens; for harmony, Ruskin and Hawthorne; for epigrammatic style, Emerson and Stephen Crane; for condensation, Bacon; for energy, Wendell Phillips, Edmund Burke, and Daniel Webster; for oratorical style, Edward Everett, William Ewart Gladstone, and other great political and pulpit speakers.

The following exercises will be found helpful:

1. Read daily two or more pages of a master of style, some of whose names have already been suggested. Do this systematically. Carefully note the selection and arrangement of words, the structure of sentences and paragraphs, the felicitous turns of expression, and other characteristics of the writer.

2. Copy in your own handwriting daily at least one page of some master stylist, carefully observing, as in your reading in the last-named exercise, special qualities in thought, word, and arrangement. Learn to "brood" over this exercise.

3. Read aloud daily two or more pages of some great oration. Take in as many words or phrases as you can with a quick glance of the eye, and speak the words to an imaginary audience. This will help you to cultivate a speaking rather than a reading style.

4. Read a page or a paragraph from some stylist, then close the book and write out the thought in your own words. Compare with the original, and note your faults.

5. As often as convenient, copy in your own handwriting some portion of a great poem by Milton, Tennyson, Byron, Wordsworth, Cowper, Bryant, or other poet.

6. Write original compositions, both in essay and oratorical form, comparing them with the work of other writers and speakers, and subjecting them to the severest criticism. Earnestly endeavor to strengthen the weak points in your style. Remember that results worth while come only from long and laborious practise.

Many excellent specimens for study, both in prose and poetry, will be found at the back of this volume. Begin your work with the following short extracts:

1. The perfect loveliness of a woman's countenance can only consist in that majestic peace which is founded in the memory of happy and useful years, full of sweet records; and from the joining of this with that yet more majestic childishness, which is still full of change and promise—opening always—modest at once, and bright, with the hope of better things to be won, and to be bestowed. There is no old age where there is still that promise.

   Thus, then, you have first to mold her physical frame, and then as the strength she gains will permit you, to fill and temper her mind with all knowledge and thoughts which tend to confirm its natural instincts of justice and refine its natural tact of love.

   All such knowledge should be given her as may enable her to understand, and even to aid, the work of men; and yet it should be given, not as knowledge—not as if it were, or could be, for her an object to know, but only to feel, and to judge. It is of no moment, as a matter of pride or perfectness in herself, whether she knows many languages or one; but it is of the utmost that she should be able to show kindness to a stranger, and to understand the sweetness of a stranger's tongue. It is of no moment to her own worth or dignity that she should be acquainted with this science or that; but it is of the highest that she should be trained in habits of accurate thought; that she should understand the meaning, the inevitableness, and the loveliness of natural laws; and follow at least some one path of scientific attainment as far as to the threshold of that bitter valley of humiliation, into which only the wisest and bravest of men can descend, owning themselves forever children, gathering pebbles on a boundless shore. It is of little consequence how many positions of cities she knows, or how many dates of events, or names of celebrated persons—it is not the object of education to turn the woman into a dictionary; but it is deeply necessary that she should be taught to enter with her whole personality into the history she reads; to picture the passages of it vitally in her own bright imagination; to apprehend, with her fine instincts, the pathetic circumstances and dramatic relations which the historian too often only eclipses by his reasoning and disconnects by his arrangement: it is for her to trace the hidden equities of divine reward, and catch Bight, through the darkness, of the fateful threads of woven fire that connect error with retribution. But chiefly of all, she is to be taught to extend the limits of her sympathy with respect to that history which is being forever determined as the moments pass in which she draws her peaceful breath, and to the contemporary calamity which, were it but rightly mourned by her, would recur no more hereafter. She is to exercise herself in imagining what would be the effects upon her mind and conduct, if she were daily brought into the presence of suffering which is not the less real because shut from her sight. She is to be taught somewhat to understand the nothingness of the proportion which that little world in which she lives and loves, bears to the world in which God lives and loves; and solemnly she is to be taught to strive that her thoughts of piety may not be feeble in proportion to the number they embrace, nor her prayer more languid than it is for the momentary relief from pain of her husband or her child, when it is uttered for the multitudes of those who have none to love them, and is "for all who are desolate and opprest."

"Sesame and Lilies." **John Ruskin**

2. Ethereal Minstrel I Pilgrim of the sky!
   Dost thou despise the earth where cares abound?
Or, while the wings aspire, are heart and eye
   Both with thy nest upon the dewy ground?
Thy nest which thou canst drop into at will,
   Those quivering wings composed, that music still !

To the last point of vision, and beyond,
   Mount, daring warbler! that love prompted strain
('Twist thee and thine a never-failing bond)
   Thrills not the less the bosom of the plain.
Yet might'st thou seem, proud privilege I to sing
   All independent of the leafy spring.

Leave to the Nightingale her shady wood:
   A privacy of glorious light is thine;
Whence thou dost pour upon the world a flood
   Of harmony, with instinct more divine;
Type of the wise, who soar, but never roam;
   True to the kindred points of Heaven and Home!

"To a Skylark." **William Wordsworth**

3. There are two classes of permanent products raised and transmitted by human activity. One of them is *cooperative* and has a parallel in the life of other creatures. As the coral-reef is deposited in increments contributed by a constant animal succession, so the city, the harbor, the aqueduct, the road enlist and attest the labors of many generations, and owe their solidity and grandeur to prolonged experience and multitudinous skill. Such

monuments record the power of the *social* spirit, and measure for us the greatness of *nations.*

The other class is purely individual and *personal,* and has no place except in human kind. An *Iliad,* an *Agamemnon,* a Divina *Commedia,* a *Hamlet,* a *Faust,* a *Madonna di San Sisto,* or a *Sinfonia Eroica* is a unique birth in which no sound mind can bear a part; and, go where it may, speak to what myriads it will, it is still an appeal of one soul to another, eliciting response as sharp and single as the echo to a solitary voice. Flowing forth from a single creative nature, it acts by its touch as an experiment in spiritual friendship, and gathers an ever-increasing group, held fast in fellowship of enthusiasm, and owing a common obligation to the genius which has discovered for them their true soul.

What and where, then, are the two members of this relation? Is the first of them nothing and nowhere? and is the homage it wrings from me paid to a blank? or to a dead book only—to blotted paper or colored canvas or an orchestral score? Heart-worship, like God, is "not of the dead, but of the living"; and that, in the thought-glance with which we look up to a Homer, a Dante, a Shakespeare, there should be no reciprocity possible —that in reverencing the prophets we do but decorate their tombs—that the touch which wakes such fires within us should be that of a *quenched* torch, would expel their chief meaning from the noblest relations subsisting among human minds.

A great, creative personality may be lonely and neglected in his day; and only when the reflection which he leaves of himself travels down the ages, does he select and gather together his natural associates and lovers: and shall he never hear the chorus of that great company, or know of that life which began for him when life had ended? Can a word that is immortal come from a speaker that is ephemeral?

"A Study of Religion." **James Martineau**

4. Whence the sound
Of instruments, that made melodious chime,
Was heard, of harp and organ; and who moved
Their stops and chords, was seen; his volant touch
Instinct through all proportions, low and high,
Fled and pursued transverse the resonant fugue.

"Paradise Lost," Book XL

Passion of sudden death! that once in youth I read and interpreted by the shadows of thy averted signs!—rapture of panic taking the shape (which among tombs in churches I have seen) of woman bursting her sepulchral bonds—of woman's Ionic form bending forward from the ruins of the grave with arching foot, with eyes upraised, with clasped, adoring hands—waiting, watching, trembling, praying for the trumpet's call to rise from dust forever! Ah, vision too fearful of shuddering humanity on the brink of mighty abysses!—vision that didst start back, that didst reel away, like a shriveling scroll before the wrath of fire racing on the wings of the wind! Epilepsy so brief of horror, wherefore is it that thou canst die? Passing so suddenly into darkness, wherefore is it that thou sheddest thy sad funeral blights upon the gorgeous mosaic of dreams? Fragments of music too passionate, heard once and heard no more, what aileth thee, that thy deep rolling chords come up at intervals through all the worlds of sleep, and after forty years, have lost no element of horror?

I

Lo, it is summer—almighty summer! The everlasting gates of life and summer are thrown open wide; and on the ocean tranquil and verdant as a savannah, the unknown lady from the dreadful vision and I myself are floating—she upon a fairy pinnace, and I upon an English three-decker. Both of us are wooing gales of festive happiness within the domain of our common country, within that ancient watery park, within that pathless chase of ocean, where England takes her pleasure as a huntress through winter and summer, from the rising to the setting sun. Ah, what a wilderness of floral beauty was hidden, or was suddenly revealed, upon the tropic islands through which the pinnace moved! And upon her deck what a bevy of human flowers—young women how lovely, young men how noble, that were dancing together, and slowly drifting toward *us* amid music and incense, amidst blossoms, from forests and gorgeous corymbi from vintages, amidst natural carolling, and the echoes of sweet girlish laughter. Slowly the pinnace nears us, gaily she hails us, and silently she disappears beneath the shadow of our mighty bows. But then, as at some signal from heaven, the music, and the carols, and the sweet echoing of girlish laughter—all are hushed. What evil has smitten the pinnace, meeting or over-taking her? Did ruin to our friends couch within our own dreadful shadow? Was our shadow the shadow of death? I looked over the bow for an answer, and, behold! the pinnace was dismantled; the revels and the revelers were found no more; the glory of the vintage was dust; and the forests with their beauty were left without a witness upon the seas. "But where," and I turned to our crew—"where are the lovely women that danced beneath the awning of flowers and clustering corymbi? Whither have fled the noble young men that danced with *them*?" Answer there was none. But suddenly the man at the masthead, whose countenance darkened with alarm, cried out, "Sail on the weather beam! Down she comes upon us; in seventy seconds she also will founder."

II

I looked to the weather side, and the summer had departed. The sea was rocking and shaking with gathering wrath. Upon its surface sat mighty mists, which grouped themselves into arches and long cathedral aisles. Down one of these, with the fiery pace of a quarrel from a crossbow, ran a frigate right athwart our coarse. "Are they mad?" some voice exclaimed from our deck. "Do they woo their ruin?" But in a moment, as she was close upon us, some impulse of a heady current or local vortex gave a wheeling bias to her course, and off she forged without a shock. As she ran past us, high aloft amongst the shrouds stood the lady of the pinnace. The deeps in malice opened ahead to receive her, the billows were fierce to catch her. But far away she was borne upon the desert spaces of the sea; while still by sight I followed her, she ran before the howl-ing gale, chased by angry seabirds and by maddening billows; still I saw her, as at the moment when she ran past us, standing amongst the shrouds, with her white draperies streaming before the wind. There she stood, with hair disheveled, one hand clutched amongst the tackling—rising, sinking, fluttering trembling, praying—there for leagues I saw her as she stood, raising at intervals one hand to heaven, amidst the fiery crests of the pursuing waves and the raving of the storm; until at last, upon a sound from afar of malicious laughter and mockery, all was hidden forever in driving showers; and afterward, but when I know not, nor how.

"Dream-Fugue." **Thomas de Quinoey**

5. The Present Age. In these brief words what a world of thought is comprehended; what infinite movements; what joys and sorrows; what hope and despair; what faith and doubt; what silent grief and loud lament; what fierce conflicts and subtle schemes of policy! what private and public revolutions! In the period through which many of us have passed, what thrones have been shaken; what hearts have bled; what millions have been butchered by their fellow-creatures; what hopes of philanthropy have been blighted! And at the same time what magnificent enterprises have been achieved; what new provinces won to science and art; what rights and liberties secured to nations! It is a privilege to have lived in an age so stirring, so pregnant, so eventful. It is an age never to be forgotten. Its voice of warning and encouragement is never to die. Its impression on history is indelible. Amidst its events, the American Revolution, the first distinct, solemn assertion of the rights of men; and the French Revolution, that volcanic force which shook the earth to its center,

are never to pass from men's minds. Over this age the night will, indeed, gather more and more as time rolls away; but in that night two forms will appear, Washington and Napoleon, the one a lurid meteor, the other a benign, serene, and undecaying star. Another American name will live in history, your Franklin; and the kite which brought lightning from heaven will be seen sailing in the clouds by remote posterity, when the city where he dwelt may be known only by its ruins. There is, however, something greater in the age than its greatest men; it is the appearance of a new power in the world, the appearance of the multitude of men on the stage where as yet the few have acted their parts alone. This influence is to endure to the end of time. What more of the present is to survive? Perhaps much of which we now take no note. The glory of an age is often hidden from itself. Perhaps some word has been spoken in our day which we have not deigned to hear, hut which is to grow clearer and louder through all ages. Perhaps there sleeps in his cradle some reformer who is to move the Church and the world, who is to open a new era in history, who is to fire the human soul with new hope and new daring. What else is to survive the age? That which the age has little thought of, but which is living in us all; I mean the soul, the immortal spirit. Of this all ages are the unfoldings, and it is greater than all. We must sot feel, in the contemplation of the vast movements in our own and former times, as if we ourselves were nothing. I repeat it, we are greater than all. We are to survive our age, to comprehend it, and to pronounce its sentence.

"The Present Age." **W.E. Channing**

6. Or stay at home, and take up one of those daily prints, which are so true a picture of the world; look down the columns of advertisements, and you will see the catalog of pursuits, projects, aims, anxieties, amusements, indulgences, which occupy the mind of man. He plays many parts: here he has goods to sell, there he wants employment; there again he

seeks to borrow money, here he offers you houses, great seats or small tenements; he has food for the million, and luxuries for the wealthy, and sovereign medicines for the credulous, and books, new and cheap, for the inquisitive. Pass on to the news of the day, and you will learn what great men are doing at home and abroad: you will read of wars and rumors of wars; of debates in the legislature; of rising men, and old statesmen going off the scene; of political contests in this city or that county; of the collision of rival interests. You will read of the money market, and the pro-vision market, and the market for metals; of the state of trade, the call for manufactures, news of ships arrived in port, of accidents at sea, of exports and imports, of gains and losses, of frauds and their detection. Go forward, and yon arrive at discoveries in art and science, discoveries (so-called) in religion, the court and royalty, the entertainments of the great, placcs of amusement, strange trials, offenses, accidents, escapes, exploits, experiments, contests, ventures. Oh, this curious, restless, clamorous, panting being which we call life! And is there to he no end to all this? Is there no object in it? It never has an end, it is forsooth its own object!

"God's Will the End of Life." **John Henry Newman**

REFERENCE

1. Qulntilian's *Institutes of Oratory, or, Education of an Orator,* Vol. 2; translated by Rev. John Selby Watson. George Bell & Sons.

6 How to Develop the Imagination

A public speaker should cultivate the habit of making vivid mental pictures of what he sees and reads. This is one of the best remedies for self-consciousness. It also develops the power of concentration, gives freshness and reality to a speaker's utterance, and greatly increases the interest of his audience. The attentive hearer keenly follows the operation of a speaker's mind, is inclined to see what he sees, and is quick to detect mental wandering away from the thought. The more vividly and accurately the speaker mentally pictures what he is saying, the more clearly and satisfactorily will his audience be imprest by his message.

Imagination, like any other faculty, can be cultivated by judicious practise. There is so much material on every hand that the public speaker will do well to choose subjects for practise such as he is likely to use. He should have special regard for mental pictures that embody harmony, beauty, and symmetry. He should endeavor to work out such pictures into the smallest detail, making them as complete as possible. This work of the imagination should become more and more selective, and less a thing of chance. Sir Benjamin Brodie says: "Physical investigation, more than anything besides, helps to teach us the actual value and right use of the imagination—of that wondrous faculty which, when left to ramble uncontrolled, leads us astray into a wilderness of perplexities and errors, a law of mists and shadows; but which, properly controlled by experience and reflection, becomes the noblest attribute to man, the source of poetic genius, the instrument of discovery in science, without the aid of which Newton would never have invented fluxions, nor Davy have decomposed the earths and alkalis, nor would Columbus have founded another continent"

Imagination may be defined as a mental image of something not present to the senses. When properly developed it enables a public speaker to summon before his mental vision experiences and observations of the past, and to live them over again. This imparts spontaneity and intensity to his words, and wins both the attention and the confidence of his audience. A well-developed imagination broadens the view of the speaker, quickens his sensibilities, and gives him a larger sympathy for mankind. If, as Carlyle says "Man carries under his hat a private theater, where as greater drama is acted than is ever performed on the mind stage, beginning and ending in eternity," how careful every one should be, and especially the public speaker, in choosing the scenes, characters, and plays to be presented there!

Begin your practise with a simple picture like the following:

1. The past rises before me like a dream. Again we are in the great struggle for national life. We hear the sounds of preparation—the music of boisterous drums—the silver voices of heroic bugles. We see thousands of assemblages, and hear the appeals of orators. We see the pale cheeks of women, and the

flushed faces of men; and in those assemblages we see all the dead whose dust we have covered with flowers. We lose sight of them no more. We are with them when they enlist in the great army of freedom. We see them part with those they love. Some are walking for the last time in quiet, woody places, with the maidens they adore. We hear the whisperings and the sweet vows of eternal love as they lingeringly part forever. Others are bending over cradles, kissing babes that are asleep. Some are receiving the blessings of old men. Some are parting with mothers who hold them and press them to their hearts again and again, and say nothing. Kisses and tears, tears and kisses; divine mingling of agony and love! And some are talking with wives, and endeavoring with brave words, spoken in the old tones, to drive from their hearts the awful fear. We see them part. We see the wife standing in the door with the babe in her arms—standing in the sunlight sobbing. At the turn of the road a hand waves—she answers by holding high in her loving arms the child. He is gone, and forever.

R.J. Ingersoll

"A Vision of War and a Vision of the Future."

Now close your eyes and recall the mental picture of what you saw and the order in which you saw it. Tell it aloud in your own words. What sounds did you hear? Describe the concourse of people you saw, the mother, the wife. Did you see the husband departing? Did you experience any feeling in reading this scene? Describe it.

Reread the extract and endeavor to get a more detailed mental impression of the picture. Again close your eyes and describe as minutely as you can just what you saw.

Repeat the exercise with the following pictures:

2. Science and revelation concur in teaching that this ball of earth, which man inhabits, is not the only

world; that millions of globes like ours roll in the immensity of space. The sun, the moon, "those seven nightly wandering fires," those twinkling stars, are worlds. There, doubtless, dwell other moral and intellectual natures, passing what man calls time, in one untired pursuit of truth and duty; still seeking, still exploring, never satisfying, never satiating, the ethereal, moral, intellectual thirst; whose delightful task it is, as it should he ours, to learn the will of the Eternal Father—to seek the good, which to that end, for them and to us who seek, hides; and finding, to admire, adore, and praise, "Him first! Him last, Him midst and without end."

Imagine one of these celestial spirits, bent on this great purpose, descending upon our globe, and led by chance to a European plain, at the point of some great battle; on which, to human eye, reckless and blind to overruling heaven, the fate of states and empires is suspended.

On a sudden, the field of combat opens on his astonished vision. It is a field which men call "glorious." A hundred thousand warriors stand in opposed ranks. Light gleams on their burnished steel. Their plumes and banners wave. Hill echoes to hill the noise of moving rank and squadron—the neigh and tramp of steeds—the trumpet, drum, and bugle call. There is a momentary pause—a silence like that which precedes the fall of a thunderbolt—like that awful stillness, which is precursor to the desolating rage of the whirlwind. In an instant, flash succeeding flash, pours columns of smoke along the plain. The iron tempest sweeps, heaping man, horse, and car in undistinguished ruin. In shouts of rushing hosts—in shock of breasting steeds—in peals of musketry—in artillery's roar—in sabers' clash—in thick and gathering clouds of smoke and dust, all human eye and ear and sense are lost. Man sees naught but the sign of onset. Man hears naught but the cry of "onward."

Not so the celestial stranger. His spiritual eye,

unobscured by artificial night, his spiritual ear, unaffected by mechanic noise, witness the real scene, naked in all its cruel horrors.

He sees lopped and bleeding limbs scattered; gashed, dismembered trunks, outspread, gore-clothed, lifeless; brains bursting from crushed skulls, blood gushing from sabered necks, severed heads, whose mouths mutter rage amidst the palsying of the last agony.

He hears the mingled cry of anguish and despair issuing from a thousand bosoms in which a thousand bayonets turn; the convulsive scream of anguish from heaps of mangled, half-expiring victims, over whom the heavy artillery wheels lumber and crush into one mass, bone and muscle and sinew, while the fet-lock of the warhorse drips with blood starting from thc last palpitation of the burst heart on which the hoof pivots.

"This is not earth"—would not such a celestial stranger exclaim?—"this is not earth, this is hell! This is not man, but demon, tormenting demon."

Thus exclaiming, would he not speed away to the skies—his immortal nature unable to endure the folly, the crime, and the madness of man?

"The Field of Battle." **Robert Hall**

3. And I saw a new heaven and a new earth: for the first heaven and the first earth are passed away; and the sea is no more. And I saw the holy city, new Jerusalem, coming down out of heaven from God, made ready as a bride adorned for her husband. And I heard a great voice out of the throne saying, Behold, the tabernacle of God is with men, and He shall dwell with them, and they shall be His peoples, and God Himself shall be with them, and be their God: and He shall wipe away every tear from their eyes; and death shall be no more; neither shall there be mourning, nor crying, nor pain, any more: the first things are passed away. And He that sitteth on the throne said, Behold, I make all things new. And

He saith, Write: for these words are faithful and true. And He said unto me, They are come to pass. I am the Alpha and the Omega, the beginning and the end. I will give unto him that is athirst of the fountain of the water of life freely. He that overcometh shall inherit these things; and I will be his God, and he shall be My son. But for the fearful, and unbelieving, and abominable, and murderers, and fornicators, and sorcerers, and idolaters, and all liars, their part shall be in the lake that burneth with fire and brimstone; which is the second death.

And there came one of the seven angels who had the seven bowls, who were laden with the seven last plagues; and he spake with me, saying, Come hither, I will show thee the bride, the wife of the Lamb. And he carried me away in the spirit to a mountain great and high, and showed me the holy city Jerusalem, coining down out of heaven from God, having the glory of God; her light was like unto a stone most precious, as it were a jasper stone, clear as crystal: having a wall great and high; having twelve gates, and at the gates twelve angels; and names written thereon, which are the names of the twelve tribes of the children of Israel: on the east were three gates; and on the north three gates; and on the south three gates; and on the west three gates. And the wall of the city had twelve foundations, and on them twelve names of the twelve apostles of the Lamb. And he that spake with me had for a measure a golden reed to measure the city, and the gates thereof, and the wall thereof. And the city lieth foursquare, and the length thereof is as great as the breadth: and he measured the city with the reed, twelve thousand furlongs: the length and the breadth and the height thereof are equal. And he measured the wall thereof, a hundred and forty and four cubits, according to the measure of a man, that is, of an angel. And the building of the wall thereof was jasper: and the city was pure gold, like unto pure glass.

The foundations of the wall of the city were adorned

with all manner of precious stones. The first foundation was jasper; the second, sapphire; the third, chalcedony; the fourth, emerald; the fifth, sardonyx; the sixth, sardius; the seventh, chrysolite; the eighth, beryl; the ninth, topaz; the tenth, chrysoprase; the eleventh, jacinth; the twelfth, amethyst. And the twelve gates were twelve pearls; each, one of the several gates was of one pearl: and the street of the city was pure gold, as it were transparent glass. And I saw no temple therein; for the Lord God the Almighty and the Lamb are the temple thereof. And the city hath no need of the sun, neither of the moon, to shine upon it: for the glory of God did lighten it, and the lamp thereof is the Lamb. And the nations shall walk amidst the light thereof: and the kings of the earth bring their glory into it. And the gates thereof shall in nowise be shut by day (for there shall be no night there): and they shall bring the glory and the honor of the nations into it: and there shall in nowise enter into it anything unclean, or be that maketh an abomination and a He: but only they that are written in the Lamb's book of life.

And he showed me a river of water of life, bright as crystal, proceeding out of the throne of God and of the Lamb, in the midst of the street thereof. And on this side of the river and on that was the tree of life, bearing twelve manner of fruits, yielding its fruit every month: and the leaves of the tree were for the healing of the nations. And there shall be no curse any more: and the throne of God and of the Lamb shall be therein: and His servants shall serve Him; and they shall see His face; and His name shall be on their foreheads. And there shall be night no more; and they need no light of lamp, neither light of sun; for the Lord God shall give them light: and they shall reign forever and ever.

Rev. xxi., xxii., 1-5. **The Bible [Am. Rev. Ver.]**

4. At the fair grounds at San Jose, California, recently, about two thousand spectators were gathered about

a balloon in which an ascension was to be made by Professor Hoff. While the balloon was being filled the professor called for several assistants, and a man by the name of Macado was one of those who stept forward. When all was ready the aeronaut called out, "Let go!" and the balloon quickly rose. As Macado endeavored-to step away he became entangled in the ropes and was lifted from the ground. He realized the peril of his situation, and as the balloon arose he took a firm hold upon the rope. The excited crowd below could hear his cries to the man in the balloon, "Save me! Save me!" The aeronaut, finding he could not draw the man up to him, decided that a descent must be made. He let the gas out of the balloon and slowly it started to descend. The young man held on to the rope with dogged determination while he was carried half a mile before he reached the ground. Many people find themselves in the course of their lives in situations where they can do nothing to help themselves, and all they can do is to stand still and trust God. The grit to hold on is a great thing. This is what Paul meant when he wrote the Ephesians about putting on the whole armor of God and then adds the words, "Having done all,... stand!"

"Pluck to Hold On." **Louis Albert Banks**

5. I visited the Garden of Gethsemane for the second time at sundown on Sunday evening. I left at a little distance my dragoman and two others, dwellers in Jerusalem, who chanced to be with us that day, that I might be alone with my thoughts, that I might read again the Scripture narrative of our Lord's agony in the garden, and that I might make the scene of His sufferings real and personal. Some have said that the present garden is not sufficiently lonely and secluded to harmonize with the descriptions given by the evangelists, and that possibly the agony of our Lord occurred in the larger garden, which existed, as it is supposed, in that day, and not in the portion of the garden now shown. But it seemed to me to be a place of peculiar loneliness and seclusion. The Mount of Olives over-hangs it on the one side

and the embattled walls of Jerusalem on the other. It is a fitting spot for one desiring to be alone with God at evening's holy hour, or under the shadows cast by the olive-trees under the light of the Passover moon. An American woman has furnished a sufficient amount of money to maintain a tank of water in the garden. This provision enables the guardians to keep the flowers constantly in bloom and the grass perpetually fresh and green. It was an admirable gift; it symbolizes the place which the garden and its sacred scenes must ever have in the minds of Christians throughout the whole world. Thoughts of wonderful tenderness came into my mind on that Sunday evening, amid the fading light of day and the gathering shadows of evening. Perhaps near the spot where I stood did Christ endure the bloody sweat of agony untold; perhaps it was here that the angel came and ministered unto Him when He was exhausted with "strong crying and tears."

> Under the olive boughs,
> Falling like ruby beads,
> The blood drops from His brows;
> He bleeds! My Savior bleeds!

Josephus tells us that the suburbs of Jerusalem abound with gardens and pleasure-grounds. The word "garden," it ought to be borne in mind, was then used with a somewhat different meaning from that which we now give to the name. The Garden of Gethsemane is now more truly a garden, in our use of the word, than it was in Christ's day. Then the word garden meant substantially what we mean by the word orchard. This garden, however, will ever be associated with but a single event, the agony of the Son of God on the evening preceding His death on the cross. Here was fulfilled the prophecy of Isaiah regarding the Christ: "I have trodden the wine-press alone." The word Gethsemane means an olive-press. The garden is but a few paces to the south from the so-called tomb of the Virgin. The entrance is from the Mount of Olives toward the southeast. The olive-oil yielded by the trees in the garden is still sold for a high price, and many rosaries are still made from the olive stones.

This garden was to me holy ground; here, if ever, I felt like taking my shoes from off my feet. Yonder, on Calvary, Christ's body was crucified; but here in Gethsemane was the crucifixion of His Soul Yonder He gave up his life; here He yielded His soul in sweet obedience to the Father's will. There the letter of the law was satisfied; here the weight of the law, in its spiritual import, fell on the soul of Christ. In this garden His "own familiar friend betrayed Him." Here the Captain of our salvation experienced the truth that the soul of His sufferings was the suffering of His soul. And here in the quiet of my own heart, at evening's holy hour, I strove to dedicate myself afresh in unswerving loyalty to my crucified Lord, and in unceasing love for the souls of men for whom IIc dicd.

Robert Stuart MacArthur

"Sunday Night Lectures on The Land and the Book."

7 Dramatic Power in Speaking

The dramatic element in speaking is by no means the exclusive property of the stage. It has its appropriate and legitimate place in, platform and pulpit delivery. The extent to which it should be employed depends upon the subject and the occasion. When properly used it is a source of great power and effectiveness.

This is not a recommendation, however, of paroxysms of feeling, wild gesticulation, tearing and combing of the hair with the fingers, violent pacing up and down the platform, and other manifestations of old-style oratory, happily now obsolete, but rather to suggest a power which, when properly used, will give life, variety, intensity, and color to the spoken message.

In reciting dramatic scenes the voice should be varied so as to faithfully impersonate each character distinctly and naturally. This affords the best kind of practise for the speaking voice.

The study of dramatic literature gives life and vividness to a speaker's style, develops his imagination, and broadens his conception of humanity. It teaches him to speak from the heart to the heart. It educates his emotions for instant use.

The effect of strong dramatic utterance is illustrated

in the story of Whitefield addressing his audience, of whom some were sailors, when he said:

"Well, my boys, we have a clear sky, and are making fine headway over a smooth sea before a light breeze, and we shall soon lose sight of land. But what means this sudden lowering of the heavens, and that dark cloud arising from beneath the western horizon? Hark! Don't you hear distant thunder? Don't you see those flashes of lightning? This is a storm gathering! Every man to his duty! How the waves rise and dash against the ship! The air is dark!—the tempest rages!—our masts are gone—the ship is on her beam-ends! What next?" This appeal instantly brought the sailors to their feet, with a shout: "The long-boat!—take to the long-boat"

This study will also give vigor and action to the speaker. The orator is not a statue, but "an animal galvanic battery on two legs," as Nathan Sheppard has it The body, the hand, the face, the eye, the mouth, all should respond to the speaker's inner thought and feeling. It should be said of him as of Wendell Phillips:

> Pure and eloquent blood
> Spoke in his cheek, and so distinctly wrought
> That one might almost say his body thought.

The public speaker should be a man of great earnestness and of strong healthy passions. These qualities can best be cultivated by the daily practising aloud of dramatic scenes. Care must be taken not to exaggerate objective effects. Gesture, facial expression, and bodily action must be subordinated to the thought.

It is said of the elder Salvini that in studying the part of *Othello,* he instructed his attendants to tie him securely to a chair, in order that he might develop his subjective expression as much as possible. When at last he appeared on the stage the critics marveled at his impersonation of a part that had almost invariably been overdone in style and action.

"All true action in the pulpit," says Doctor Kennard, "must first proceed from the soul. In other words, it has a psychic base and spring. If the man's soul is in a healthy and vigorous state, inspired by his theme, his thought will swim to the surface and reflect itself in his physical features and organs. By a subtle psychological law the whole nervous and muscular system responds to the sympathetic impulses of the emotions and will; feeling and purpose mysteriously and spontaneously press at every gate of the eyes, the lips, the cheeks, the hands, the feet, for *expression*. The preacher's heart, swelling with inspired energetic conviction and emotion, lifts itself up like a great tidal wave, overflows its banks and pours itself forth in expressions of the features, glances of the eyes, quivering of the mouth, tones of the voice and movements of the limbs, so that the physical structure becomes simply the complex and delicate organ of expression for the brain, and heart, and will."[1]

The emotions of the speaker must first be awakened, then judiciously trained to respond instantly to his demands. They must first be intelligently controlled that they may be safely and unconsciously liberated at the moment of use in public speaking. Shakespearian numbers are particularly recommended because of their scope and fidelity.

The following scenes will give material for practise of this kind. Further selections will be found in the latter part of the book.

KING HENRY VIII

Act III, Scene 2—Wolsey After His Fall

Scene: *An antechamber in Henry VIII.'s palace.*

Wel. So, farewell to the little good you bear me.
Farewell! a long farewell, to all my greatness!
This is the state of man; today he puts forth
The tender leaves of hope; tomorrow blossoms,
And bears his blushing honors thick upon him;
The third day comes a frost, a killing frost,
And, when he thinks, good easy man, full surely
His greatness is a-ripening, nips his root,
And then he falls, as I do. I have ventur 'd,
Like little wanton boys that swim on bladders,
This many summers in a sea of glory,
But far beyond my depth; my high-blown pride
At length broke under me, and now has left me
Weary and old with service, to the mercy
Of a rude stream, that must forever hide me.
Vain pomp and glory of this world, I hate ye;
I feel my heart new-opened. Oh, how wretched
Is that poor man that hangs on princes' favors!
There is, betwixt that smile we would aspire to,
That sweet aspect of princes, and their ruin,
More pangs and fears than wars or women have;
And when he falls, he falls like Lucifer,
Never to hope again.

Enter Cromwell

Why, how now, Cromwell?
Crom. I have no power to speak, sir.
Wol. What! amazed
At my misfortunes? can thy spirit wonder
A great man should decline? Nay, an you weep,
I am fall'n indeed.
Crom. How does your grace?
Wol. Why, well;
Never so truly happy, my good Cromwell.
I know myself now; and I feel within me
A peace above all earthly dignities,

A still and quiet conscience. The king has cur'd me,
I humbly thank his grace; and from these shoulders,
These ruin'd pillars, out of pity, taken
A load would sink a navy—too much honor;
Oh, 'tis a burden, Cromwell, 'tis a burden
Too heavy for a man that hopes for heaven!

Crom. I am glad your grace has made that right use of it.

Wol. I hope I have; I am able now, methinks,
(Out of a fortitude of soul I feel,)
To endure more miseries and greater far
Than my weak-hearted enemies dare offer.
What news abroad?

Crom. . The heaviest and the worst
Is your displeasure with the king.

Wol. God bless him!

Crom. The next is, that Sir Thomas More is chosen
Lord Chancellor in your place.

Wol. That's somewhat sudden;
But he's a learned man. May he continue
Long in his highness' favour, and do justice
For truth's sake and his conscience; that his bones,
When he has run his course and sleeps in blessings,
May have a tomb of orphans' tears wept on 'em!
What more?

Crom. That Cranmer is return'd with welcome,
Install'd Lord Archbishop of Canterbury.

Wol. That's news indeed.

Crom. Last, that the Lady Anne,
Whom the king hath in secrecy long married,
This day was view'd in open as his queen,
Going to chapel; and the voice is now
Only about her coronation.

Wol. There was the weight that pull'd me down.
O Cromwell!
The king has gone beyond me; all my glories
In that one woman I have lost forever.
No sun shall ever usher forth mine honors,
Or gild again the noble troops that waited
Upon my smiles. Go, get thee from me, Cromwell;
I am a poor fall 'n man, unworthy now
To by thy lord and master. Seek the king;
That son, I pray, may never set! I have told him

What and how true thou art; he will advance thee;
Some little memory of me will stir him—
I know his noble nature—not to let
Thy hopeful service perish too; good Cromwell,
Neglect him not; make use now, and provide
For thine own future safety.

Crom. O my lord,
Must I, then, leave yon? must I needs forego
So good, so noble, and so true a master?
Bear witness, all that have not hearts of iron,
With what a sorrow Cromwell leaves his lord.
The king shall have my service; but my prayers
Forever and forever shall be yours.

Wol. Cromwell, I did not think to shed a tear
In all my miseries; but thou hast fore 'd me,
Out of thy honest truth, to play the woman.
Let's dry our eyes; and thus far hear me, Cromwell;
And, when I am forgotten, as I shall be,
And sleep in dull cold marble, where no mention
Of me more must be heard of, say, I taught thee,
Say, Wolsey, that once trod the ways of glory,
And sounded all the depths and shoals of honor,
Found thee a way, out of his wreak, to rise in;
A sure and safe one, tho thy master miss 'd it.
Mark but my fall, and that which ruin'd me.
Cromwell, I charge thee, fling away ambition!
By that sin fell the angels; how can man, then,
The image of his Maker, hope to win by it?
Love thyself last; cherish those hearts that hate thee;
Corruption wins not more than honesty.
Still in thy right hand carry gentle peace,
To silence envious tongues. Be just, and fear not;
Let all the ends thou aim 'st at be thy country's,
Thy God's and truth's; then, if thou fall'st, O Cromwell,
Thou fall'st a blessed martyr! Serve the king;
And,—prithee lead me in;
There take an inventory of all I have,
To the last penny; 'tis the king's; my robe,
And my integrity to Heaven, are all
I dare not call mine own. O Cromwell, Cromwell!
Had I but serv'd my God with half the zeal
I served my king, He would not in mine age

Have left me naked to mine enemies!
Crom. Good sir, have patience.
Wol So I have. Farewell
The hopes of court! my hopes in heaven do dwell. *[Exeunt.*

HENRY V

Part of Act IV

Enter Chorus

Chorus. Now entertain conjecture of a time,
When creeping murmur, and the poring dark,
Fills the wide vessel of the universe.
From camp to camp, through the foul womb of night,
The hum of either army stilly sounds,
That the fix'd sentinels almost receive
The secret whispers of each other's watch:
Fire answers fire; and through their paly flames
Each battle sees the other's umber'd face:
Steed threatens steed, in high and boastful neighs
Piercing the night's dull ear; and from the tents,
The armorers, accomplishing the knights,
With busy hammers closing rivets up,
Give dreadful note of preparation.
The country cocks do crow, the clocks do toll,
And the third hour of drowsy morning name.
Proud of their numbers, and secure in soul,
The confident and overlusty French
Do the low-rated English play at dice:
And chide the cripple tardy-gaited night,
Who, like a foul and ugly witch, doth limp
80 tediously away. The poor condemned English,
Like sacrifices, by their watchful fires
Sit patiently, and inly ruminate
The morning's danger; and their gesture sad,
Investing lank-lean cheeks, and war-worn coats,
Presenteth them unto the gazing moon
So many horrid ghosts. Oh, now, who will behold
The royal captain of this ruin'd band,
Walking from watch to watch, from tent to tent,
Let him cry—Praise and glory on his head!
For forth he goes, and visits all his host;
Bids them good-morrow with a modest smile;

And calls them brothers, friends, and countrymen.
Upon his royal face there is no note,
How dread an army hath enrounded him;
Nor doth he dedicate one jot of color
Unto the weary and all-watched night:
But freshly looks, and overbears attaint
With cheerful semblance, and sweet majesty;
That every wretch, pining and pale before,
Beholding him, plucks comfort from his looks;
A largess universal, like the sun,
His liberal eye doth give to every one,
Thawing cold fear that, mean and gentle all,
Behold, as may unworthiness define,
A little touch of Harry in the night.
And so our scene must to the battle fly;
Where, (O for pity!) we shall much disgrace—
With four or five most vile and ragged foils,
Right ill-disposed in brawl ridiculous—
The name of Agincourt: Yet, sit and see;
Minding true things by what their mockeries be.

[Exit.

Scene: *The English camp. Characters: The Dukes of* Gloster *and* Bedford, *the King's brothers, the Earls of* West-Moreland, Salisbrury, Exeter, *and others.*

West. Of fighting men they have full threescore thousand.
Exe. There's five to one; besides, they all are fresh.
Sal. God's arm strike with us! 'tis a fearful odds.
God be wi' you, princes all; I'll to my charge:
If we no more meet, till we meet in heaven,
Then, joyfully—my noble lord of Bedford—
My dear lord Gloster,—and my good lord Exeter,—
And my kind kinsman,—warriors all, adieu!
Bed. Farewell, good Salisbury; and good luck go with thee.

[Exit Salisbury

Enter King Henry

West. O that we now had here
But one ten thousand of those men in England,
That do no work today!
K. Hen. What's he that wishes so?
My cousin Westmoreland?—No, my fair cousin:

If we are mark'd to die, we are enough
To do our country loss; and if to live,
The fewer men, the greater share of honor.
God's will! I pray thee, wish not one man more.
By Jove, I am not covetous for gold;
Nor care I who doth feed upon my cost;
It yearns me not if men my garments wear;
Such outward things dwell not in my desires:
But if it be a sin to covet honor,
I am the most offending soul alive.
No, 'faith, my coz, wish not a man from England :
God's peace! I would not lose so great an honor,
As one man more, methinks, would share from me,
For the best hope I have. O, do not wish one more :
Bather proclaim it, Westmoreland, through my host,
That he which hath no stomach to his fight,
Let him depart, his passport shall be made,
And crowns for convoy put into his pursc :
We would not die in that man 's company,
That fears his fellowship to die with us.
This day is call'd the feast of Crispian:
He that outlives this day, and comes safe home,
Will stand a tiptoe when this day is nam'd,
And rouse him at the name of Crispian.
He that shall live this day, and see old age,
Will yearly on the vigil feast his neighbors,
And say tomorrow is Saint Crispian :
Then will he strip his sleeve, and show his scars,
And say, these wounds I had on Crispian's day.
Old men forget; yet all shall be forgot,
But he'll remember, with advantages,
What feats he did that day! Then shall our names,
Familiar in his mouth as household words—
Harry the king, Bedford and Exeter,
Warwick and Talbot, Salisbury and Gloster, —
Be in their flowing eups freshly remember'd :
This story shall the good man teach his son;
And Crispin Crispian shall ne'er go by,
From this day to the ending of the world,
But we in it shall be remembered;
We few, we happy few, we band of brothers :
For he, today, that sheds his blood with me,

Shall be my brother; be he ne'er so vile,
This day shall gentle his condition :
And gentlemen in England, now a-bed,
Shall think themselves accurst, they were not here;
And hold their manhoods cheap, whiles any speaks,
That fought with us upon Saint Crispian's day.

Enter Salisbury

Sal. My sovereign lord, bestow yourself with speed,
The French are bravely in their battles set,
And will with all expedience charge on us.
K. Hen. All things are ready, if our minds be so.
West. Perish the man whose mind is backward now!
K. Hen. Thou dost not wish more help from England, cousin?
West. God's will, my liege, would you and I alone,
Without more help, could fight this royal battle!
K. Hen. Why, now thou hast unwish'd five thousand men;
Which likes me better, than to wish us one.—
You know your places; God be with you all!

Tucket. Enter Montjoy

Mont. Once more I come to know of thee, King Harry,
If for thy ransom thou wilt now compound,
Before thy most assured overthrow?
For, certainly, thou art so near the gulf,
Thou needs must be englutted. Besides, in mercy,
The Constable desires thee thou wilt mind
Thy followers of repentance; that their souls
May make a peaceful and a sweet retire
From off these fields, where (wretches) their poor bodies
Must lie and fester.
K. Hen. Who hath sent thee now?
Mont. The Constable of France.
K . Hen. I pray thee, bear my former answer back;
Bid them achieve me, and then sell my bones.
Good God I why should they mock poor fellows thus?
The man that once did sell the lion's skin
While the beast lived, was kill'd with hunting him.
A many of our bodies shall, no doubt,
Find natives' graves : upon the which, I trust,
Shall witness live in brass of this day's work;
And those that leave their valiant bones in France,

Dying like men, tho buried in your dunghills,
They shall be famed; for there the sun shall greet them,
And draw their honors reeking up to heaven;
Let me speak proudly,—Tell the Constable,
We are hut warriors for the working day:
Our gayness and our gilt are all besmirch'd
With rainy marching in the painful field;
There's not a piece of feather in our host,
(Good argument, I hope, we will not fly,)
And time hath worn us into slovenry:
But, by the mass, our hearts are in the trim:
And my poor soldiers tell me, yet ere night
They'll be in fresher robes: or they will pluck
The gay new coats o'er the French soldiers' heads,
And turn them out of service. If they do this,
(As, if God please, they shall,) my ransom then
Will soon be levied. Herald, save Thou thy labor,
Come Thou no more for ransom, gentle herald;
They shall have none, I swear, hut these my joints:
Which if they have as I will leave 'em them,
Shall yield them little, tell the Constable.

Mont. I shall, King Harry. And so fare thee well:
Thou never shalt hear herald any more. [*Exit.*

K. Hen. I fear, thou'lt once more come again for ransom.

Enter the Duke or York

York. My Lord, most humbly on my knees I beg
The leading of the vaward.

K. Hen. Take it, brave York.—Now, soldiers, march away;—
And how thou pleasest, God, dispose the day!

[*Exeunt.*

Scene: *The field of battle. Characters: Captain* Gower, an *English captain, and Captain* Fluellen, *a Welsh captain.*

Flu. Kill the poys and the luggage I 'tis expressly against the law of arms: 'tis as arrant a piece of knavery, mark you now, as can be offert in the 'orld: In your conscience now, is it not?

Gow. 'Tis certain there's not a boy left alive; and the cowardly rascals that ran from the battle have done this slaughter: besides, they have burned and carried away all that was in the king's tent; wherefore the king, most worthily, hath caused every soldier to cut his prisoner's throat. O, 'tis a gallant king!

Flu. Ay, he was porn at Monmouth, Captain Gower: What call you the town's name, where Alexander the pig was porn?

Flu. Alexander the Great?

Flu. Why, I pray you, is not pig great? The pig, or the great, or the mighty, or the huge, or the magnanimous, are all one reckonings, save the phrase is a little variations.

Goto. I think Alexander the Great was born in Macedon; his father was called Philip of Macedon, as I take it.

Flu. I think it is in Macedon where Alexander is porn. I tell you, captain,—if you look in the maps of the 'orld, I warrant, you shall find in the comparisons between Macedon and Monmouth, that the situations, look you, is both alike. There is a river in Macedon; and there is also moreover a river at Monmouth; it is called Wye, at Monmouth; but it is out of my prains, what is the name of the other river; but 'tis all one, 'tis alike as my fingers is to my fingers, and there is salmons in both. If you mark Alexander's life well, Harry of Mon-mouth's life is come after it indifferent well; for there is figures in all things. Alexander, (God knows, and yon know,) in his rages, and his furies, and his wraths, and his cholers, and his moods, and his displeasures, and his indignations, and also being a little intoxicates in his prains, did, in his ales and his angers, look you, kill his pest friend, Clytus,

Gow. Our king is not like him in that; he never killed any of his friends.

Flu. It is not well done, mark yon now, to take the tales out of my mouth, ere it is made an end and finished. I speak but in the figures and comparisons of it: As Alexander is kill his friend Clytus, being in his ales and his cups; so also Harry Monmouth, being in his right wits and his goot judgments; is turn away the fat knight with the great pelly-doublet: he was full of jests, and gipes, and knaveries, and mocks; I am forget his name.

Gow. Sir John Falstaff.

Flu. That is he: I can tell you, there is goot men porn at Monmouth.

Gow. Here comes his majesty.

Alarum. *Enter* King Henry *with a part of the English forces;* Warwick, Gloster, Exeter, *and others.*

K. Hen. I was not angry since I came to France,
Until this instant.—Take a trumpet, herald;
Ride thou unto the horsemen on yon hill;
If they'll do neither, we will come to them;
Or void the field; they do offend our sight:
If they'll do neither, we will come to them;
And make them skirr away as swift as stones
Enforced from the old Assyrian slings:
Besides, we'll cat the throats of those we have;
And not a man of them, that we shall take,
Shall taste our Mercy :— Go, and tell them so.

Enter Montjoy

Exe. Here comes the herald of the French, my liege.
Glo. His eyes are humbler than they used to be.
K. Hen. How now? what means this, herald? know'st thou not,
That I have fined these bones of mine for ransom?
Com'st thou again for ransom?
Mont. No, great king:
I come to thee for charitable license,
That we may wander o'er this bloody field,
To book our dead, and then to bury them:
To sort our nobles from our common men;
For many of our princes (wo the while!)
Lie drown'd and soak'd in mercenary blood;
(So do our vulgar drench their peasant limbs
In blood of princes; and their wounded steeds
Fret, fetlock deep in gore, and, with wild rage,
Yerk out their armed heels at their dead masters,
Killing them twice.) 0 give us leave, great king,
To view the field in safety, and dispose
Of their dead bodies.
K. Hen. I tell thee truly, herald,
I know not, if the day be ours, or no;
For yet a many of your horsemen peer,

And gallop o'er the field.

Mont. The day is yours.

K. Hen. Praised be God, and not our strength for it!
What is this castle call'd, that stands hard by?

Mont. They call it Agincourt.

K. Hen. Then we call this the field of Agincourt,
Fought on the day of Crispin Crispians.

SCENES FROM "THE RIVALS"

By Richard B. Sheridan

Act II, Scene I

Capt A. Now for a parental lecture. I hope he has heard nothing of the business that has brought me here. I wish the goat had held him fast in Devonshire, with all my soul!

Enter Sir Anthony

Capt. A. Sir, I am delighted to see yon here, and looking BO well!—your sudden arrival at Bath madc me apprehensive for your health.

Sir A. Very apprehensive, I dare say, Jack.—What, you are recruiting here, hey?

Capt. A. Yes, sir, I am on duty.

Sir A. Well, Jack, I am glad to see you, tho I did not expect it; for I was going to write to you on a little matter of business.—Jack, I have been considering that I grow old and infirm, and shall probably not trouble you long.

Capt. A. Pardon me, sir, I never saw you look more strong fend hearty, and I pray fervently that you may continue so.

Sir A. I hope your prayers may be heard, with, all my heart. Well, then, Jack, I have been considering that as I am so strong and hearty, I may continue to plague you for a long time.—Now, Jack, I am sensible that the income of your commission, and what I have hitherto allowed you, is but a small pittance for a lad of your spirit.

Capt. A. Sir, you are very good.

Sir A. And it is my wish, while yet I live, to have my boy make some figure in the world.—I have resolved, therefore, to fix you at once in a noble independence.

Capt. A. Sir, your kindness overpowers me.—Yet, sir, I presume you would not wish me to quit the army?

Sir A. Oh! that shall be as your wife chooses.

Capt. A. My wife, sir!

Sir A. Ay, ay, settle that between you,—settle that between you.

Capt. A. A. wife, sir, did you say?

Sir A. Ay, a wife: why, did not I mention her before?

Capt. A. Not a word of her, sir.

Sir A. Oddso! I mustn't forget her, tho.—Yes, Jack, the independence I was talking of is by a marriage,—the fortune is saddled with a wife,—but, I suppose, that makes no difference?

Capt. A. Sir! sir!.you amaze me!

Sir A. Why, what's the matter with the fool? Just now you were all gratitude and duty.

Capt A. I was sir,—you talked to me of independence and a fortune, hut not a word of a wife.

Sir A. Why, what difference does that make? Odds life, sir! if you have the estate, you must take it with the live stock on it, as it stands.

Capt. A. Pray, sir, who is the lady?

Sir A. What's that to you sir?—Come, give me your promise to love, and to marry her directly.

Capt. A. Sure, sir, this is not very reasonable, to summon my affections for a lady I know nothing of!

Sir A. I am sure, sir, 'tis more unreasonable in you to object to a lady you know nothing of.

Capt. A. You must excuse me, sir, if I tell you, once for all, that in this point I can not obey you.

Sir A. Harkye, Jack!—I have heard you for some time with patience—I have been cool—quite cool; but take care—you know I am compliance itself—when I am not thwarted; no one more easily led—when I have my own way;—but don't yon put me in a frenzy.

Capt. A. Sir, I must repeat it—in this, I can not obey you.

Sir A. Now, hang me, if ever I call you Jack again while I live!

Capt. A. Nay, sir, but hear me.

Sir A. Sir, I won't hear a word—not a word! not one word! so give me your promise by a nod—and I'll tell you what, Jack—I mean, you dog—if you don't, by—

Capt. A. What, sir, promise to link myself to some mass of ugliness!

Sir A. Zounds! sirrah I the lady shall be as ugly as I choose: she shall have a hump on each shoulder; she shall be as crooked as the crescent; her one eye shall roll like the bull's in Cox's Museum; she shall have a skin like a mummy,—she shall be all this, sirrah!—yet I'll make you ogle her all day, and sit up all night, to write sonnets on her beauty.

Capt. A. This is reason and moderation indeed!

Sir A. None of your sneering, puppy! no grinning, jackanapes!

Capt. A. Indeed, sir, I never was in a worse humor for mirth in my life.

Sir A. 'Tis false, sir; I know you are laughing in your sleeve; I know you'll grin when I am gone, sirrah!

Capt. A. Sir, I hope I know my duty better.

Sir A. None of your passion, sir! none of your violence, if you please. It won't do with me, I promise you.

Capt. A. Indeed, sir, I never was cooler in my life.

Sir A. 'Tis a lie!—I know you are in a passion in your

heart; I know you are, you hypocritical young dog; but it won't do.

Capt. A. Nay, sir, upon my word—

Sir A, So you will fly out! Can't you be cool, like me!—What good can passion do?—passion la of no service, you impudent, insolent, overbearing reprobate!—There, you sneer again!—don't provoke me!—but-yon rely upon the mildness of my temper—you do, you dog! You play upon the meekness of my disposition! Yet take cure—the patience of a saint may be overcome at last!—but mark!—I give you six hours and a half to consider of this; if you then agree, without any condition, to do everything on earth that I choose, why—confound you, I may in time forgive yon. If not, zounds! don't enter the same hemisphere with me! don't dare to breathe the same air, or use the same light with me; but get an atmosphere and a sun of your own! I'll strip you of your commission; I'll lodge a five-and-three-pence in the hands of trustees, and yon shall live on the interest. I'll disown you; I'll disinherit you, and, hang me! if ever I call yon Jack again!

[Exit.

Capt. A. Mild, gentle, considerate father! I kiss your hands.

II

Act III, Scene 1

Capt. A. Tis just as Fag told me, indeed!—Whimsical enough, 'faith! My father wants to force me to marry the very girl I am planning to run away with I He must not know of my connection with her yet awhile. He has too summary a method of proceeding in these matters; however, I'll read my recantation instantly. My conversion is something sudden, indeed; but I can assure him it is very sincere.

Enter Sir Anthony

Sir A. No—I'll die sooner than forgive him! Die, did I say? I'll live these fifty years to plague him. At our last meeting his impudence had almost put me out of temper—an obstinate, passionate, self-willed boy! Who can he take after? This is my return for putting him, at twelve years old, into a marching regiment, and allowing him fifty pounds a year, besides his pay, ever since! But I have done with him—he's anybody's son for me—I never will see him more—never—never—never—never.

Capt. A. Now for a penitential face!

Sir A. Fellow, get out of my way!

Capt. A. Sir, you see a penitent before you.

Sir A. I see an impudent scoundrel before me.

Capt. A. A sincere penitent. I am come, sir, to acknowledge my error and to submit entirely to your will.

Sir A. What's that?

Capt. A, I have been revolving, and reflecting, and considering on your past goodness, and kindness, and condescension to me.

Sir A. Well, sir!

Capt. A. I have been likewise weighing and balancing what you were pleased to mention concerning duty, and obedience, and authority.

Sir A. Why, now, you talk sense, absolute sense; I never heard anything more sensible in my life. Confound you, you shall be Jack again!

Capt. A. I *am.* happy in the appellation.

Sir A. Why, then, Jack, my dear Jack, I will now inform you who the lady really is. Nothing but your passion and violence, you silly fellow, prevented me telling you at first. Prepare, Jack, for wonder and rapture—prepare! What think you of Miss Lydia Languish?

Capt.A. Languish! What, the Languishes of Worcestershire?

Sir A. Worcestershire! No! Did you never meet Mrs, Malaprop and her niece, Miss Languish, who came into our country just before you were last ordered to your regiment?

Capt. A. Malaprop! Languish! I don't remember ever to have heard the name before. Yet stay: I think I do recollect something. Languish—Languish! She squints, don't she! A little red-haired girl?

Sir A. Squints! A red-haired girl! Zounds, no!

Capt A. Then I must have forgot: it can't be the same person.

Sir A. Jack, Jack! what think you of blooming, love-breathing seventeen?

Capt. A. As to that, sir, I am quite indifferent; if I can please you in the matter, 'tis all I desire.

Sir A. Nay, bat Jack, such eyes! such eyes! so innocently wild! so bashfully irresolute! Not a glance but speaks and kindles some thought of love! Then, Jack, her cheeks! her cheeks, Jack! so deeply blushing at the insinuations of her tell-tale eyes! Then, Jack, her lips! Oh, Jack, lips, smiling at their own discretion! and, if not smiling, more sweetly pouting—more lovely in sullenness! Then, Jack, her neck! Oh, Jack! Jack!

Capt. A. And which is to be mine, sir, the niece or the aunt?

Sir *A.* Why, you unfeeling, insensible puppy, I despise you! When I was of your age, such a description would have made me fly like a rocket! The aunt, indeed! Odds life! when I ran away with your mother, I would not have touched anything old or ugly to gain an empire!

Capt. A. Not to please your father, sir?

Sir A. To please my father—zounds! not to please—Oh! my father? Oddso! yes, yes! if my father, indeed, had desired—that's quite another matter. Tho he wasn't the indulgent father that I am, Jack.

Capt. A. I dare say not, sir.

Sir A. Bat, Jack, you axe not sorry to find your mistress is BO beautiful?

Capt. A. Sir, I repeat it, if I please you in this affair, 'tis all I desire. Not that I think a woman the worse for being handsome; but, sir, if you please to recollect, you before hinted something about a hump or two, one eye, and a few more graces of that kind. Now, without being very nice, I own I should rather choose a wife of mine to have the usual number of limbs, and a limited quantity of back; and tho one eye may be very agreeable, yet, as the prejudice has always run in favor of two, I would not wish to affect a singularity in that article.

Sir A. What a phlegmatic sot it is! Why, sirrah, you are an anchorite! a vile, insensible stock! You a soldier! you're a walking block, fit only to dust the company's regimentals on! Odds life, I've a great mind to marry the girl myself!

Capt. A. I am entirely at your disposal, sir, if you should think of addressing Miss Languish yourself, I suppose you would have me marry the aunt; or if you should change your mind, and take the old lady, 'tis the same to me—I'll marry the niece.

Sir A. Upon my word, Jack, thou art either a very great hypocrite, or—but, come, I know your indifference on such a subject must be all a lie—I'm sure it must. Come, now, hang your demure face; come, confess, Jack, you have been lying, haven't you? You have been playing the hypocrite, hey! I'll never forgive you, if you haven't been lying and playing the hypocrite.

Capt. A. I am sorry, sir, that the respect and duty which I bear to you should be so mistaken.

Sir A. Respect and duty! But come along with me. I'll write a note to Mrs. Malaprop, and you shall visit the lady directly. Her eyes shall be the Promethean torch to you—come along, I'll never forgive you if you don't come back stark mad with rapture and impatience—if you don't, 'egad, I'll marry the girl myself. *[Exeunt.*

8 How to Train the Memory

The extemporaneous style of delivery should be the ultimate aim of every public speaker. To this end the memory should be cultivated to the highest possible degree. Many persons despair because of their poor and unreliable memories, but they are unwilling to give the time and practise necessary to develop them. There is no royal road to this as to any other branch of study. The memory can be cultivated, however, by any one having the necessary perseverance and application.

Memory is largely a matter of association of ideas. If we cultivate the habit of being *interested,* we are at the same time strengthening the memory. Memory depends upon securing vivid first impressions. These come through concentration, and we concentrate when we are sufficiently interested.

There are numerous so-called "memory systems," but the objection usually offered to them is that the end does not justify the means. If the average student had sufficient time and patience to carry the exercises to completion, he would doubtless be greatly benefited, but in most cases he soon becomes disheartened and gives up his study before any substantial results are possible.

What constitutes a good memory? One might answer,

the ability to recall accurately and instantly the greatest number of things at the moment of need. A well-trained memory, then, may be likened unto a series of pigeonholes, in which knowledge may be found so systematized as to make it easily available.

If the memory be poor it will be helpful at first to inquire into the reason for this condition. Such questions may be asked as: Is it lack of proper practise? Is it due to ill health? Is it lack of observation or of interest? Is there a systematic plan of gathering and recording knowledge? Are the daily habits of thinking and reading well-ordered? Is there lack of thoroughness, accuracy, and deliberateness? These and similar questions should be answered frankly, and a determined effort made to correct such faults as are noted.

To strengthen the memory it is advisable to form the habit of making comparisons and contrasts. In reading a book one should take notes and at the first opportunity try to repeat from memory, to some other person, the general ideas of what has been read. It is helpful also to interrogate one's self as to what has been seen or read. A good exercise is to read a passage from some writer and endeavor to repeat the same ideas in different words and in as many ways as possible. Vivid picturing of the thought helps to impress it upon the mind, and frequent repetition of a passage or speech will gradually fix it in the memory.

Committing to heart each day a verse or prose extract will train the memory with surprizing rapidity. An exercise that has been used with good results is to enter a room, take a quick glance around, walk out, and write down what you remember of the things that you have seen. The same exercise can be applied to passing a shop-window.

The following selections are suggested for memorizing, the student taking a passage for each day. He may indefinitely extend the list at his own taste and discretion.

1. Let every dawn of morning be to you as the beginning of life, and every setting sun be to you as its close. Then let every one of these short lives leave its sure record of some kindly thing done for others; some goodly strength or knowledge gained for yourself.

John Ruskin.

2. The day returns and brings us the petty round of irritating concerns and duties. Help us to play the man, help us to perform them with laughter and kind faces; let cheerfulness abound with industry. Give us to go blithely on our business all this day, bring us to our resting beds weary and content and undishonored, and grant us in the end the gift of sleep.

"Morning Prayer." **Robert Louis Stevenson.**

3. Let no soft slumber close my eyes,
Ere I have recollected thrice
The train of actions through the day.
Where have my feet marked out their way?
What have I learnt where'er I've been,
From all I've heard, from all I've seen?
What know I more that's worth the knowing?
What have I done that's worth the doing?
What have I sought that I should shun?
What duties have I left undone,
Or into what new follies run?
These self-inquiries are the road
That leads to virtue and to God.

"Self-Inquiry." ***From the Greek of*** **Pythagoras.**

4. A little thing, a sunny smile,
A loving word, at morn,

And all day long the sun shone bright,
The cares of life were made more light,
  And sweetest hopes were born.
A little thing, a hasty word,
  A cruel frown, at morn,
And aching hearts went on their way
And toiled throughout a dreary day,
  Disheartened, sad and lorn.

"In the Morning." **Anonymous**

5. Do not keep the alabaster boxes of your love and tenderness sealed up until your friends are dead. Fill their lives with sweetness. Speak approving, cheering words while their care can hear them and while their hearts can be thrilled and made happier; the kind things you mean to say when they are gone, say before they go. The flowers you mean to send for their coffin, send to brighten and sweeten their homes before they leave them. If my friends have alabaster boxes laid away, full of fragrant perfumes of sympathy and affection, which they intend to break over my body, I would much rather that they would bring them out in my weary and troubled hours, and open them, that I may be refreshed and cheered while I need them. I would rather have a plain coffin, without a flower, a funeral without a eulogy, than a life without the sweetness of love and sympathy. Let us learn to anoint our friends beforehand for their burial. Post-mortem kindness does not cheer the burdened spirit. Flowers on the coffin cast no fragrance backward over the weary way.

Anonymous

6. Now Love is the remedy, the great sweetener of the mind and body. It produces harmony, and harmony is equilibrium-health.

   This must first be established in the mind through belief and trust in the Infinite Love, and Omnipresent Good, then the practise of love and self-forgetfulness toward others.

   If we would attract love to ourselves, we must feel it

for others, and make ourselves lovable; and that should be our whole concern, to love more and more, and think less and less of self; then we will grow sweet and wholesome, and fragrant as a flower. The blood will be pure and rich, and filled with vitality, and, in short, all things will become new, for the former things will have passed away.

"Spiritual Realizations." **Florence Willard day**

7. So live that when thy summons comes to join
The innumerable caravan that moves
To that mysterious realm, where each shall take
His chamber in the silent halls of death,
Thou go not, like the quarry slave at night,
Scourged to his dungeon, but, sustained and soothed
By an unfaltering trust, approach thy grave
Like one who wraps the drapery of his coach
About him, and lies down to pleasant dreams.

"Thanatopsis." **William Cullen Bryant**

8. Some men employ their health, an ugly trick,
In making known how oft they have been sick.
And give us in recitals of disease,
A doctor's trouble, but without the fees;
Relate how many weeks they kept their bed,
How an emetic or cathartic sped:
Nothing is slightly touched, much less forgot.
Nose, ears, and eyes seem present on the spot.
Now the distemper, spite of draft or pill,
Victorious seemed, and now the doctor's skill;
And now,—alas, for unforeseen mishaps!
They put on a damp nightcap and relapse:
They thought they must have died, they were so bad;
Their peevish hearers almost wish they had.

"Descanting on Illness." **William Cowper**

9 Power of Illustration

A story well-told, or an illustration that illustrates, gives an added power to public speaking. Illustrations not only stimulate the imagination of the hearer, but also move the heart and arouse special interest. Appropriateness, clearness, and fluency are essential to successful story-telling. Hesitation, lack of memory, and irrelevancy invariably invite disaster. It is not always necessary nor desirable that a story be memorized and repeated in exact words, but the thought and the order of the thought, as well as the particular points to be made, should be clearly fixed in the mind. It is good practise to rehearse a story several times, endeavoring to vary the phraseology.

Some one has likened illustrations unto windows that let the light in. Because of their concrete character they make a strong and direct appeal to the hearer, touching, as they usually do, his personal experience. For this reason illustrations should be chosen, whenever possible, upon subjects that are familiar to the audience. There must, however, be something to illustrate. Stories introduced merely for their own sake, or to fill up gaps, or to disguise poverty of thought, are undesirable and ineffective. Phillips Brooks goes further and says: "We confine too much the office of illustration if we give it only the duty of making truth clear to the understanding and do not also allow it the privilege of making truth glorious to the imagination."

Abstract philosophy and close argument, if long continued in speech, become wearisome to an audience. They demand some relief. A good illustration, skillfully introduced, rests the mind of the listener, lends variety and vivacity to the speaker's style, and drives home his message with increased effectiveness.

Henry Ward Beecher owed much of his power and success to his resourcefulness in this respect He says:

"The effect of illustrations upon ideality is very great. They bring into play the imaginative faculty, which is only another name for ideality. Now all great truth is beautiful. It carries in it elements of taste and fitness. The 'beauty of holiness' we find spoken of in the Word of God, and this is a beauty that does not belong to anything material God is transcendently a lover of beauty, and all the issues of the divine soul are, if we could see them as He sees them, beautiful, just as self-denial and love are beautiful, and as purity and truth and all good things are beautiful."

"It is not, therefore, in the interest of truth that a man should sift it down to the merest bare nuggets of statement that it is susceptible of; and this is not best for an audience. It is best that a truth should have argument to substantiate it, and analysis and close reasoning; yet when you come to give it to an audience you should clothe it with flesh, so that it shall be fit for their understandings. In no other way can you so stir up that side of the mind to grasp your statements and arguments easily, and prepare it to remember them. You can not help your audience in any other way so well as by keeping alive in them the sense of the imagination and making the truth palpable to them, because it is appealing to the taste, to the sense of the beautiful in imagery as well as to the sense of truth."

A speaker's illustrations should be as new and as varied as possible. Objection is sometimes raised to compilations of stories for illustration, on the ground that they soon become hackneyed. But this need not be the case if the speaker recasts the story in his own words and gives it a new application. The sources for material of this character are numerous. In addition to the regular collections of stories, the daily newspapers, magazines and other periodicals offer an almost inexhaustible supply of suggestions. The Bible itself is a storehouse of illustration and parable. Personal observation, however, will give the public speaker his best and most valuable material for illustration. Such material will not only have the quality of originality, but will palpitate with life and freshness, coming directly out of everyday human experience. The speaker should cultivate the habit of closely observing and noting things he sees around him. He should accustom himself to the exercise of mentally describing such things to himself, and at the first opportunity he should tell them to another. In this way the habit will gradually become an unconscious one, and the speaker will seldom feel at a loss for illustrative material.

It is well to keep two special books, one in which to write every story to be preserved for future use, the other in which to paste printed clippings.

The following extracts are intended to be suggestive. Those that the speaker wishes to use should be committed to memory, and repeated aloud in varied language as already mentioned.

1. You remember that in Prussia there was a law which exempted the only son of a widow from going to war but it is said that so closely were they driven at one time for recruits, that the law was for a time rescinded, and the widow's only son was taken. Suppose such a thing happened here, and there should be a widow whose only son was demanded of her. See her come forward, saying, "Ay, take him; my country is dearer to me even than he is." She puts him forward, and says, "Go forth, my son, to die if it be necessary; I give thee up, I give thee willingly. "You see the red, red eye of the widow; she hath wiped it dry, but she hath wept in secret; and if we steal behind the door when her son is gone, and see her pouring out whole floods of sorrow, we can tell how great must have been her love for her country which made her give up him— her all. Beloved, we never should know Christ's love in all its heights and depths if He had not died; nor could we tell the Father's deep affection if He had not given His Son to die.

Louis Albert Banks

"Spurgeon's Illustrative Anecdotes."

2. During a heavy storm off the coast of Spain, a dismasted merchantman was observed by a British frigate drifting before the gale. Every eye and glass were on her, and a canvas shelter on a deck almost level with the sea suggested the idea that there yet might be life on board. With all his faults, no man is more alive to humanity than the rough and hardy mariner; and so the order instantly sounds to put the ship about, and presently a boat puts off with instructions to bear down upon the wreck. Away after that drifting hulk go these gallant men through the swell of a roaring sea; they reach it; they shout; and now a strange object rolls out of that canvas screen against the lee shroud of a broken mast. Hauled into the boat, it proves to be the trunk of a man, bent head and knees together, so dried and shriveled as to be hardly felt within the ample clothes, and so light that a mere boy lifted it on board. It is laid on the deck; in horror and pity the crew gather round it; it shows

signs of life; they draw nearer; it moves, and then mutters—mutters in a deep, sepulchral voice—*"There is another man."* Saved him-self, the first use the saved one made of speech was to seek to save another. Oh! learn that blest lesson. Be daily practising it And so long as in our homes, among our friends, in this wreck of a world which is drifting down to ruin, there lives an unconverted one, there is *"another man"* let us go to that man and plead for Christ; go to Christ and plead for that man; the cry, "Lord save me, I perish, changed into one as welcome to i a Savior's ear, 'Lord save them, they perish.' "

"The Messenger." **Thomas Guthrie**

3. I will show you three fools. One is yonder soldier, who has been wounded on the field of battle, grievously wounded, well nigh unto death; the surgeon is by his side, and the soldier asks him a question. Listen, and judge of his folly. What question does he ask? Does he raise his eyes with eager anxiety and inquire if the wound be mortal, if the practitioner's skill can suggest means of healing, or if the remedies are within reach and the medicine at hand ? No, nothing of the sort; strange to tell, he asks, "Can you inform me with what sword I was wounded and by what Russian I have been thus grievously mauled? I want," he adds, "to learn every minute particular respecting the origin of my wound." The man is delirious or his head is affected. Surely such questions at such a time are proof enough that he is bereft of his senses.

   There is another fool. The storm is raging, the ship is flying impetuous before the gale, the dark scud moves swiftly over head, the masts are creaking, the sails are rent to rags, and still the gathering tempest grows more fierce. Where is the captain? Is he busily engaged on the deck, is he manfully facing the danger, and skillfully suggesting means to avert it? No, sir, he has retired to his cabin, and there with studious thoughts and crazy fancies he is speculating on the place where this storm took its rise. "It is mysterious, this wind; no one ever yet," he says, "has been able to discover it." And so he, reckless of the vessel, the lives of the passengers, and his own life, is careful only to solve his curious questions. The man is mad, sir; take the rudder from his hand; he is clean gone mad! If he should ever run on shore, shut him up as a hopeless lunatic.

The third fool I shall doubtless find among yourselves. Yon are sick and wounded with sin, yon are in the storm and hurricane of Almighty vengeance, and yet the question which you would ask of me this morning would be, "Sir, what is the origin of evil?" You are mad, air, spiritually mad.

Louis Albert Banks

"Spurgeon's Illustrative Anecdotes."

4. I remember once riding from Buffalo to the Niagara Falls. I said to a gentleman,' "What river is that, sir?"

"That," he said, "is Niagara River."

"Well, it is a beautiful stream," said I; "bright and fair and glassy. How far off are the rapids?"

"Only a mile or two," was the reply.

"Is it possible that only a mile from us we shall find the water In the turbulence which it must show near the falls?"

"You will find it so, sir." And so I did find it; and the first sight of Niagara I shall never forget.

Now launch your bark on that Niagara River; it is bright, smooth, beautiful and glassy. There is a ripple at the bow; the silver wake you leave behind adds to your enjoyment. Down the stream you glide, oars, sails and helm in proper trim, and you set out on your pleasure excursion.

Suddenly some one cries out from the bank:

"Young men, ahoy!"

"What is it?"

"The rapids are below you."

"Ha! ha! we have heard of the rapids; but we are not such fools as to get there. If we go too fast, then we shall up with the helm and steer to the shore; we will get the mast in the socket, and hoist the sail, and speed to the land. Then on, boys; don't be alarmed, there is no danger."

"YOUNG MEN, AHOY

"What is it?"

"BEWARE! BEWARE! THE RAPIDS ARE BELOW YOU!"

Now yon see the water foaming all around. See how fast you pass that point! Up with the helm! Now turn! Pull hard! *Quick!* QUICK! QUICK! Pull *hard for your lives!* Pull till the blood starts from your nostrils and the veins start like whipcords upon your brow! Set the mast in the socket! hoist the sail! ah! ah! it is too late! *"Shrieking,* HOWLING, BLASPHEMING, *over they go!"*

Thousands go over the rapids of intemperance every year through *the power of habit,* crying all the while: "When I find out that it is injuring me, I will give it up!"

"The Power of Habit." **John B. Gough.**

5. I read a story the other day of some Russians crossing wide plains studded over here and there with forests. The villages were ten or a dozen miles from each other, the wolves were out, the horses were rushing forward madly, the travelers could hear the baying of the wolves behind them; and, tho the horses tore along with all speed, yet the wolves were fast behind, and they only escaped, as we say, "by the skin of their teeth," managing just to get inside some hut that stood in the road, and to shut to the door. Then they could hear the wolves leap on the roof; they could hear them dash against the sides of the hut; they could hear them gnawing at the door, and howling, and making all sorts of dismal noises; but the travelers were safe, because they had entered in by the door, and the door was shut. Now, when a man is in Christ, he can hear, as it were, the devils howling like wolves, all fierce and hungry for him; and his own sins, like wolves, are seeking to drag him down to destruction. But he has got in to Christ, and that is such a shelter that all the devils in the world, if they were to come at once, could not start a single beam of that eternal refuge; it must stand fast, tho the earth and heaven

should pass away. Now, to every man and woman Christ says that if they have entered in by the door, they shall be saved.

Selected. **Spurgeon**

6. The dissipations of social life are blasting and destroying a vast multitude. With many life is a masquerade ball, and as at such entertainments gentlemen and ladies put on the garb of kings and queens, or mountebanks or clowns, and at the close put off the disguise, so a great many pass their whole life in a mask, taking off the mask at death. While the masquerade ball of life goes on, they trip merrily over the floor, gemmed hand is stretched to gemmed hand, gleaming brow bends to gleaming brow. On with the dance! Flush and rustle and laughter of immeasurable merrymaking. But after a while the languor of death comes on the limbs and blurs the eyesight. Lights lower. Floor hollow with sepulchral echo. Music saddened into a wail. Lights lower. Now the maskers are only seen in the dim light. Now the fragrance of the flowers is like the sickening odor that comes from garlands that have lain long in the vaults of cemeteries. Lights lower. Mists gather in the room. Glasses shake as tho quaked by sullen thunder. Sight caught in the curtain. Scarf drops from the shoulder of beauty a shroud. Lights lower. Over the slippery boards in dance of death glide jealousies, envies, revenges, lust, despair and death. Stench of lamp-wicks almost extinguished. Torn garlands will not half cover the ulcerated feet. Choking damps. Chilliness. Feet still. Hands closed. Voices hushed. Eyes shut. Lights out.

"Lights Out." **T. Dewttt Talmage**

7. One of our railroad engineers, some years since, was running an express train of ten filled cars. It was in the night, and a very dark night too. His train was behind time, and he was putting the engine to the utmost speed of which it was capable, in order to reach a certain point at the proper hour. He was running on a straight and level track, and at this unusual

velocity, when a conviction struck him that he must stop.

'A something seemed to tell me," he said, "that to go ahead was dangerous, and that I must stop if I would save life. I looked back at my train and it was all right, I strained my eyes and peered into the darkness, and could see no signal of danger, nor anything betokening danger, and there, in the day-time, I could have seen five miles. I listened to the working of my engine, tried the water, looked at the gage, and all was right. I tried to laugh myself out of what I considered a childish fear; but, like Banquo's ghost, it would not down at my bidding, but grew stronger in its hold upon me, I thought of the ridicule I would have heaped upon me if I did stop; but it was all of no avail. The conviction—for by this time it had ripened into a conviction—that I must stop, grew stronger, and I resolved to do so. I shut off, and blew the whistle for brakes accordingly. I came to a dead halt, got off, and went ahead a little way without saying anything to anybody what was the matter. I had a lamp in my hand, and had gone but about sixty feet when I saw what convinced me that premonitions are sometimes possible. I dropt the lantern from my nerveless grasp and sat down on the track utterly unable to stand."

He goes on to tell that there some one had drawn a spike which had long fastened a switch rail, and opened a switch which always had been kept locked, which led on to a track—only about one hundred and fifty feet long—which terminated in a stone quarry !

"Here it was, wide open, and had I not obeyed my premonitory warning—call it what you will—I should have run into it, and at the end of the track, only about ten rods long, my heavy engine and train, moving at the rate of forty-five miles an hour, would have come into collision with a solid wall of rock eighteen feet high! The consequences, had I done so, can neither be imagined nor described, but they could by no possibility have been otherwise than fatally horrible."

"A Prmonition." **Anonymous**

8. "Do you see this lock of hair?" said an old man to me.

"Yes; but what is it? It is, I suppose, a curl from the head of a dear child long since dead."

"It is not. It is a lock of my own hair; and it is now nearly seventy years since it was cut from this head."

"But why do you prize a lock of your own hair so much!"

"It has a story belonging to it, a strange one. I keep it thus with care because it speaks to me more of God, and of His special care, than anything else I possess. I was a little child of four years old, with long curly locks, which in the sun, or rain, or wind, hung down my cheeks uncovered. One day my father went into the woods to cut up a log, and I went with him. I was standing a little way behind him, or rather at his side, watching with interest the strokes of the heavy ax as it went up and came down upon the wood, sending off splinters with every stroke, in all directions. Some of the splinters fell at my feet, and I eagerly stooped to pick them up. In doing so I stumbled forward, and in a moment my curly head lay upon the log, I had fallen just at the moment when the ax was coming down with all its force. It was too late to stop the blow. Down came the ax. I screamed, and my father fell to the ground in terror. He could not stay the stroke, and in the blindness which the sudden horror caused, he thought he had killed his boy. We soon recovered— I from my fright, and he from terror. He caught me in his arms, and looked at me from head to foot to find the deadly wound which he was sure he had inflicted. Not a drop of blood nor a scar was to be seen. He knelt upon the grass and gave thanks to a gracious God. Having done so, he took up his ax, and found a few hairs upon its edge. He turned to the log he had been splitting, and there was a single curl of his boy's hair, sharply cut through and laid upon the wood. How great the escape! It was as if an angel had turned aside the edge at the moment it was descending upon my head.

"That lock he kept all his days as a memorial of God's care and love. That lock he left me on his death-bed.

I keep it with care. It tells me of my father's God and mine. It rebukes unbelief and ahum. It bids me trust Him forever. I have had many tokens of fatherly love in my threescore yean and ten, but somehow this speaks most to my heart. It is the oldest and perhaps the most striking. It used to speak to my father's heart; it now speaks to mine."

"The Lock of Hair." **Anonymous**

9. Last summer I saw Moscow, in some respects the most splendid city under the sun. The emperor afterward asked me if I had seen it, for Moscow is the pride of Russia. I told him yes, and that I had seen Moscow burn. I will tell you what I meant. After examining nine hundred brass cannons which were picked out of the snow after Napoleon retreated from Moscow, each cannon deep cut with the letter "N," I as-cended a tower of some two hundred and fifty feet, just before sunset, and on each platform there were bells, large and small, and I climbed up among the bells, and then, as I reached the top, all the bells underneath me began to ting, and they were joined by the bells of fourteen hundred towers and domes and turrets. Some of the bells sent out a faint tinkle of sound, a sweet tintinnabulation that seemed a bubbling of the air, and others thundered forth boom after boom, boom after boom, until it seemed to shake the earth and fill the heavens—sounds so weird, so sweet, so awful, so grand, so charming, so tremendous, so soft, so rippling, so reverberating—and they seemed to wreathe and whirl and rise and sink and burst and roll and mount and die. When Napoleon saw Moscow burn, it could not have been more brilliant than when I saw the fourteen hundred turrets aflame with the sunset; and there were roofs of gold, and walls of malachite, and pillars of porphyry, and balustrades of mosaic, and architecture of all colors mingling the brown of autumnal forests and the blue of summer heavens, and the conflagration of morning skies, and the emerald of rich grass, and the foam of tossing seas. The mingling of so many sounds was an entrancement almost too much for

human nerves and human eyes and human ears. I expect to see nothing to equal it until you and I see heaven. But that will surpass it and make the memory of what I saw that July evening in Moscow almost tame and insipid. All heaven aglow and all heaven a-ring, not in the sunset, but in the sunrise. Voices of our own kindred mingling with the doxologies of empires. Organs of eternal worship responding to the trumpets that have wakened the dead. Nations in white. Centuries in coronation. Anthems like the voice of many waters. Circle of martyrs. Circle of apostles. Circle of prophets. Thrones of cherubim. Thrones of seraphim. Throne of archangel. Throne of Christ. Throne of God. Thrones! Thrones! Thrones! The finger of God points that way. Stop not until you reach that place. Through the atoning Christ, all I speak of and more may be yours and mine. Do you not now hear the chime of the bells of that metropolis of the universe! Do you not see the shimmering of the towers? Good-morning.

"The Bells of Moscow." **T. De Witt Talmage**

Velpean, the eminent French surgeon, successfully performed a perilous operation on a five-year-old child. The mother, over-joyed, called upon him and said:

"Monsieur, I do not know how to express my gratitude. May I present you, however, with this pocketbook, embroidered with my own hands?"

"Madam," said Velpean, "my art is not merely a matter of feeling. My life has its necessities, like yours. Allow me to decline your charming gift and request a more substantial remuneration."

"But, monsieur, what do you wish? Fix the fee yourself."

"Five thousand francs, madam."

She quietly opened the pocketbook, which contained ten one-thousand-franc notes, counted out five, and politely handing them to Velpean, retired.

Anonymous

10 Power in Conversation

Conversation offers one of the best and most practical helps to the study of public speaking. Here common faults of speech can be readily noted, and habits of fluent and natural expression established. The facility and self-confidence gained here will be valuable in speaking before an audience.

Probably nothing betrays a man so unmistakably as his style of conversation. The quality of his voice, his use of words, his ability to put his ideas into forceful and effective speech, all disclose his breeding and education. The value of conversation as an educational force is emphasized by President Eliot, of Harvard, who says: "I recognize but one mental acquisition as an essential part of the education of a lady or gentleman, namely, an accurate and refined use of the mother-tongue." Dr. Nicholas Murray Butler, of Columbia, says: "First among the evidences of an education I name correctness and precision in the use of the mother-tongue."

The best public speaking and preaching of today is mainly colloquial or conversational in style. Hence conversation offers the best models for study and practise. The ability to speak to the point, to describe vividly a recent journey, or to tell an interesting story, is a practical and direct preparation for the larger work of public address. The practise of communicating to others what one has seen or heard, will gradually awaken a desire to speak before a larger audience.

The conversation of children often serves as the best model of easy unaffected speech. Their vivacity and genuineness might well be copied by those who wish to move and influence men.

The student of public speaking should be careful not to indulge at any time in loose and incorrect speech. In his daily conversation he should exercise the utmost care in pronouncing every word clearly and correctly, in pure-toned voice, and usually in a low key. He should avoid everything that is slipshod in speech, high pitch, rapid rate, half-closed mouth, and the disposition to be vociferous.

Dr. Richard Storrs, the gifted and eloquent preacher, has recommended conversation as one of the best means of refreshing the mind and replenishing it with active force. He says: "Conversation, if practised as it ought to be, as a commerce of thought between responsive and interchanging minds, is an invaluable aid toward gaining the art of easy and self-possest public speech. I do not think we have as much of it as we ought, or that it holds the place which it should in our plans of life, as a real educational force. It is much the same exercise, if you analyze it, as public speaking. Of course it is not the same altogether. In public speech your utterance of thought is more prolonged; it is monolog not dialog. You miss the help which comes from interjected remarks or replies; and you are not so immediately conscious of the sympathy or the collision of the adjacent minds. Still, conversation is much the same form of mental activity, and it always helps the public speaker. It trains the mind to think rapidly, and to formulate thought with facility and success; and each sense of such success, which is gained in conversation, will give one more confidence when he stands before an audience.

The following extracts in conversational style will serve as introductory practise along these lines. They should be read aloud, with natural and spontaneous expression, and with due regard to clear and correct enunciation.

1. "I am willing to amuse you if I can, sir; quite willing; but I can not introduce a topic, because how do I know what will interest you? Ask me questions, and I will do my best to answer them."

"Then, in the first place, do you agree with me that I have a right to be a little masterful, abrupt, perhaps exciting sometimes, on the grounds I stated—namely, that I am old enough to be your father, and that I have battled through a varied experience with many men of many nations, and roamed over half the globe, while you have lived quietly with one set of people in one house?"

"Do as you please, sir."

"That is no answer; or rather, it is a very irritating, because a very evasive one; reply clearly."

"I don't think, sir, you have a right to command me, merely because you are older than I, or because you have seen more of the world than I have; your claim to superiority depends on the use you have made of your time and experience."

"Humph! Promptly spoken. But I won't allow that, seeing that it would never suit my case, as I have made an indifferent, not to say a bad use of both advantages. Leaving superiority out of the question then, you must still agree to receive my orders now and then, without being piqued or hurt by the tone of command—will you?"

I smiled: I thought to myself Mr. Rochester *is* peculiar—he seems to forget that he pays me 30 pounds per annum for receiving his orders.

"The smile is very well," said he, catching instantly the passing expression; "but speak, too."

"I was thinking, sir, that very few masters would trouble themselves to inquire whether or not their paid subordinates were piqued and hurt by their orders."

"Paid subordinates I What, you are my paid subordinate, are you? Oh, yes, I had forgotten the salary! Well, then, on that mercenary ground, will you agree to let me hector a little?"

"No, sir, not on that ground, but on the ground that you did forget it, and that yon care whether or not a dependent is comfortable in his dependency, I agree heartily."

"And will you consent to dispense with a great many conventional forms and phrases, without thinking that the omission arises from insolence?"

"I am sure, sir, I should never mistake informality for insolence : one I rather like, the other nothing free-born would submit to even for a salary."

"Humbug! Most things free-born will submit to anything for a salary; therefore keep to yourself, and don't venture on generalities of which you are intensely ignorant. However, I mentally shake hands with you for your answer, despite its inaccuracy, and as much for the manner in which it was said as for the substance of the speech. The manner was frank and sincere; one does not often see such a manner; no, on the contrary, affectation, or coldness, or stupid, coarse-minded misapprehension of one's meaning are the usual rewards of candor. Not three in three thousand raw school-girl governesses would have answered me as you have just done. But I don't mean to flatter you; if you are cast in a different mold to the majority, it is no merit of yours: Nature did it. And then, after all, I go too fast in my conclusions; for what I yet know, you may be no better than the rest; you have intolerable defects to counterbalance your few good points."

"And so may you," I thought. My eye met his as the idea crossed my mind. He seemed to read the glance, answering as if its import had been spoken as well as imagined—

"Yes, yes, you are right," said he; "I have plenty of faults of my own: I know it, and I don't wish to palliate them, I assure you. God wot, I need not be too severe about others; I have a past existence, a series of deeds, a color of life to contemplate within my own breast which might well call my sneers and censures from my neighbors to myself. I started, or rather (for, like other defaulters, I like to lay half the blame on ill fortune and adverse circumstances), was thrust on to a wrong tack at the age of one-and-twenty, and have never recovered the right course since: bat I might have been very different; I might have been as good as you—wiser—almost as stainless. I envy you your peace of mind, your clean conscience, your unpolluted memory. Little girl, a memory without Wot or contamination must be an exquisite treasure—an inexhaustible source of pure refreshment: is it not ?"

"How was your memory when you were eighteen, sir?"

"All right then; limpid, salubrious: no gush of bilge-water had turned to fetid puddle. I was your equal at eighteen— quite your equal. Nature meant me to be on the whole a good man, Miss Eyre: one of the better kind; and you see I am not so. You would say yon don't see it: at least I flatter myself I read as much in your eye (beware, by the by, what you express with that organ, I am quick at interpreting its language). Then, take my word for it, I am not a villian; you are not to suppose that—not to attribute to me any such bad eminence; bat owing, I verily believe, rather to circumstances than to my natural bent, I am a trite, common place sinner, hackneyed in all the poor petty dissipations with which the rich and worthless try to put on life. Do you wonder that I avow this to you? Know that in the course of your future life you will often find yourself elected the involuntary confidante of your acquaintances' secrets: people will instinctively find out, as I have done, that it is not your forte to tell of yourself, hut to listen while others talk of themselves; they will feel, too, that you listen with no malevolent scorn of their indiscretion, but with a kind of innate sympathy, not the less comforting and encouraging because it is very unobtrusive in its manifestations."

"How do you know?—how can you guess all this, sir?"

"I know it well; therefore I proceed almost as freely as if I were writing my thoughts in a diary. You would say, I should have been superior to circumstances: so I should—so I should; bat you see I was not. When fate wronged me, I had not the wisdom to remain cool: I turned desperate; then I de-generated. Now, when any vicious simpleton excites my disgust by his paltry ribaldry, I can not flatter myself that I am better than he: I am forced to confess that he and I are on a level. I wish I had stood firm—God knows I do! Dread remorse when you are tempted to err, Miss Eyre: remorse is the poison of life."

"Repentance is said to be its cure, sir."

"It is not its cure. Reformation may be its cure; and I could reform—I have strength yet for that—if—but where is the use of thinking of it, hampered, burdened, curst as I am? Besides, since happiness is irrevocably denied me, I have a right to get pleasure out of life; and I *will* get it, cost what it may."

"Then you will degenerate still more, sir."

"Possibly: yet why should I, if I can get sweet, fresh pleasure? And I may get it as sweet and fresh as the wild honey the bee gathers on the moor."

"It will sting—it will taste bitter, sir."

"How do you know?—you never tried it. How very serious—how very solemn you look; and you are as ignorant of the matter as this cameo head" (taking one from the mantelpiece). "You have no right to preach to me, you neophyte, that have not passed the porch of life, and are absolutely unacquainted with its mysteries."

"I only remind you of your own words, sir: you said error brought remorse, and you pronounced remorse the poison of existence."

"And who talks of error now? I scarcely think the notion that flitted across my brain was an error. I believe it was an inspiration rather than a temptation: it was very genial, very soothing—I know that. Here it comes again! It is no devil, I assure you; or if it be, it has put on the robes of an angel of light. I think I must admit so fair a guest when it asks entrance to my heart."

From "Jane Eyre." **Charlotte Bronte**

2. Altho he had arrived at his journey's end for the day at noon, he had since insensibly walked about the town so far and so long that the lamplighters were now at their work in the streets and the shops were sparkling up brilliantly. Thus reminded to turn toward his quarters, he was in the act of doing so, when a very little hand crept into his and a very little voice said:

"Oh, if you please, I am lost!"

He looked down, and saw a very little fair-haired girl.

"Yes," she said, confirming her words with a serious nod. "I am, indeed. I am lost."

"What is your name?"

"Polly."

"What is your other name?"

The reply was prompt but unintelligible.

Imitating the sound, as he caught it, he hazarded the guess, "Trivits?"

"Oh, not" said the child, shaking her head. "Nothing like that."

"Say it again, little one."

An unpromising business. For this time it had quite a different sound.

He made the venture: "Paddens?"

"Oh no!" said the child, "Nothing like that."

"Once more. Let us try it again, dear."

A most hopeless business. This time it swelled into four syllables. "It can't be Tappitarver?" said Barbox Brothers, rubbing his head with his hat in discomfiture.

"No! It ain't," the child quietly assented.

On her trying this unfortunate name once more, with extraordinary efforts at distinctness, it swelled into eight syllables at least.

"Ah! I think," said Barbox Brothers, with a desperate air of resignation, "that we had better give it up."

"But I am lost," said the child nestling her little hand more closely in his, "and you'll take care of me, won't you?"

If ever a man were disconcerted by division between compassion on the one hand, and the very imbecility of irresolution on the other, here the man was. "Lost!" he repeated, looking down at the child. "I am sure I am. What is to be done!"

"Where do you live?" asked the child, looking up at him wistfully.

"Over there," he answered, pointing vaguely in the direction of the hotel.

"Hadn't we better go there?" said the child.

"Really," he replied, "I don't know but what we had."

So they set off, hand in hand—he, through comparison of himself against hi little companion, with a clumsy feeling on him as if he had just developed into a foolish giant; she, clearly elevated in her own tiny opinion by having got him BO neatly out of his embarrassment.

"We are going to have dinner when we get there, I suppose?" said Polly.

"Well," he rejoined, "I—yes, I suppose we are."

"Do you like your dinner?" asked the child.

"Why, on the whole," said Barbox Brothers, "yes, I think I do."

"I do mine," said Polly. "Have you any brothers and sisters?"

"No, have you!"

"Mine are dead."

"Oh!" said Barbox Brothers. With that absurd sense of unwieldiness of mind and body weighing him down, he would not have known how to pursue the conversation beyond this curt rejoinder, but that the child was always ready for him.

"What," she asked, turning her soft hand coaxingly in his, "are you going to do to amuse me after dinner?"

"Upon my soul, Polly," exclaimed Barbox Brothers, very much at a loss, "I have not the slightest idea!"

"Then I tell you what," said Polly. "Have you got any cards at the house?"

"Plenty," said Barbox Brothers, in a boastful vein.

"Very well. Then I'll build houses, and you shall look at me. You mustn't blow, you know."

"Oh no!" said Barbox Brothers. "No, no, no! No blowing! Blowing's not fair."

He flattered himself that he had said this pretty well for an idiotic monster; but the child, instantly perceiving the awkward- ness of his attempt to adapt himself to her level, utterly destroyed his hopeful opinion of himself by saying, compassionately: "What a funny man you are!"

Feeling, after this melancholy failure, as if he every minute grew bigger and heavier in person and weaker in mind, Barbox gave himself up for a bad job. No giant ever submitted more meekly to be led in triumph by all-conquering Jack, than he to be bound in slavery to Polly.

"Do you know any stories?" she asked him.

He was reduced to the humiliating confession: "No."

"What a dunce you must be, mustn't you?" said Polly.

He was reduced to the humiliating confession: "Yes."

"Would you like me to teach you a story? But you must remember it, you know, and be able to tell it right to somebody else afterward?"

He professed that it would afford him the highest mental gratification to be taught a story, and that he would humbly endeavor to retain it in his mind. Whereupon Polly, giving her hand a new little turn in his, expressive of settling down for enjoyment, commenced a long romance, of which every relishing clause began with the words: "So this," or "And so this," As, "So this boy"; or, "So this fairy"; or, "And so this pie was four yards round and two yards and a quarter deep." The interest of the romance was derived from the intervention of this fairy to punish this boy for having a greedy appetite. To achieve which purpose, this fairy made this pie, and this boy ate and ate and ate and his cheeks swelled and swelled and swelled. There were many tributary circumstances, but the forcible interest culminated in the total consumption of the pie and the bursting of this boy. Truly he was a fine sight, Barbox Brothers, with serious attentive face, an ear bent down, much jostled on the pavements of the busy town, but afraid of losing a single incident of the epic, lest he should be examined in it by and by and found deficient.

"Barbox Brothers & Go." **Charles Dickens**

3. We took possession of the private box assigned to us: and Mrs. Fletcher seated herself in the place of honor—each of the young ladies taking it by turns to occupy the other corner. Miss Minny and Master Jones occupied the middle places; and it was pleasant to watch the young gentleman throughout the performance of the comedy—during which he was never quiet for two minutes—now shifting his chair, now swinging to and fro upon it, now digging his elbows into the capacious aides of Mrs. Captain Flather, now beating with his boots against the front of the box or trampling upon the skirts of Mrs. Flather's satin garment.

He occupied "himself unceasingly, too, in working up and down Mrs. F's double-barreled French opera-glass—not a little to the detriment of that instrument and the wrath of the owner; indeed, I have no doubt that had not Mrs. Flather reflected that Mrs. Colonel Jones gave some of the most elegant parties in London, to which she was very anxious to be invited, she would have boxed Master

Augustine's ears in the presence of the whole audience of Covent Garden.

One of the young ladies was, of course, obliged to remain in the back row with Mr. Spec. We could not see much of the play over Mrs. F's turban; but I trust we were not unhappy in our retired position. O Miss Emily! 0 Miss Louisa I there is one who would be happy to sit for a week close by either of you, tho it were on one of those abominable little private-box chairs, I know, for my part, that every time the box-keeperess popped in her head, and asked if we would take any refreshment, I thought the interruption odious.

Our young ladies, and their stout chaperon and aunt, had come provided with neat little bouquets of flowers, in which they evidently took a considerable pride, and which were laid, on their first entrance, on the ledge in front of our box.

But presently, on the opposite side of the house, Mrs. Cutbush, of Pocklington Gardens, appeared with her daughters, and bowed in a patronizing manner to the ladies of our party, with whom the Cutbash family had a slight acquaintance.

Before ten minutes, the bouquets of our party were whisked away from the ledge of the box. Mrs. Flather dropt hers to the ground, where Master Jones's feet speedily finished it; Miss Louisa Twigg let hers fall into her lap, and covered it with her pocket-handkerchief. Uneasy signals passed between her and her sister. I could not, at first, understand what event had occurred to make these ladies so unhappy.

At last the secret came out The Misses Cutbash had bouquets like little haystacks before them. Our small nosegays, which had quite satisfied the girls until now, had become odious in their little jealous eyes; and the Cutbushes triumphed over them.

I have joked the ladies subsequently on this adventure; but not one of them will acknowledge the charge against them. It was mere accident that made them drop the flowers—pure accident. They jealous of the Cutboshes—

not they, indeed; and, of course, each person on this head is welcome to his own opinion.

How different, meanwhile, was the behavior of my young friend Master Jones, who is not as yet sophisticated by the world. He not only nodded to his father's servant, who had taken a place in the pit, and was to escort his young master home, but he discovered a school-fellow in the pit likewise. "By Jove, there's Smith!" he cried out, as if the sight of Smith was the most extraordinary event in the world. He pointed out Smith to all of us. He never ceased nodding, wink-ing, grinning, telegraphing, until he had succeeded in attracting the attention not only of Master Smith, but of the greater part of the house; and whenever anything in the play struck him as worthy of applause, he instantly made signals to Smith below, and shook his fist at him, as much as to say, "By Jove, old fellow, ain't it good? I say, Smith, isn't it prime, old boy?" He actually made remarks on his fingers to Master Smith during the performance.

I confess he was one of the best night's entertainment to me. How Jones and Smith will talk about that play when they meet after holidays! And not only then will they remember it, but all their lives long. Why do you remember that play you saw thirty years ago, and forget the one over which you yawned last week? "Ah, my brave little boy," I thought in my heart, "Twenty years hence you will recollect this, and have forgotten many a better thing. You will have been in love twice or thrice by that time, and have forgotten it; you will have buried your wife and forgotten her; you will have had ever so many friendships and forgotten them. You and Smith won't care for each other, very probably; but you'll remember all the actors and the plot of this piece we are seeing."

I protest I have forgotten, it myself. In. Our back row we could not see or hear much of the performance (and no great loss)—fitful bursts of elocution only occasionally reaching us, in which we could recognize the well-known nasal twang of the excellent Mr. Stupor, who performed the part of the young hero; or the ringing laughter of Mrs. Belmore, who had to giggle through the whole piece.

It was one of Mr, Boyster's comedies of English life.

Frank Nightrake (Stupor) and his friend Bob Fitzoffley appeared in the first scene, having a conversation with that impossible valet of English comedy, whom any gentleman would turn out-of-doors before he could get through half a length of the dialog assigned. I caught only a glimpse of this act. Bob, like a fashionable young dog of the aristocracy (the character was played by Bulwer, a meritorious man, but very stout, and nearly fifty years of age), was drest in a rhubarb-colored body-coat with brass buttons, a couple of under-waistcoats, a blue satin stock with a paste brooch in it, and an eighteen-penny cane, which he never let out of his hand, and with which he poked fun at everybody. Frank Nightrake, on the contrary, being at home, was attired in a very close-fitting chintz dressing-gown, lined with glazed red calico, and was seated before a large pewter teapot, at breakfast. And, as your true English comedy is the representation of nature, I could not but think how like these figures on the stage, and the dialog which they used, were to the appearance and talk of English gentlemen of the present day.

The dialog went on somewhat in the following fashion:

Bob Fitzoffley (enters whistling).—"The top of the morning to thee, Frank I What! at breakfast already? At chocolate and the *Morning Post,* like a dowager of sixty? Slang *(he pokes the servant with his cane),* what has come to thy master, thou Prince of Valets! thou pattern, of Slaveys 1 thou swiftest of Mercuries! Has the Honorable Francis Nightrake lost his heart, or his head, or his health?"

Frank (laying down the paper).—"Bob, Bob, I have lost all three! I have lost my health, Bob, with thee and thy like, over the Burgundy at the club; I have lost my head, Bob, with thinking how I shall pay my debts; and I have lost my heart, Bob, oh, to such a creature!"

Bob.—"A Venus, of course?"

Slang.—"With the presence of Juno."

Bob.—"And the modesty of Minerva."

Frank.— "And the coldness of Diana."

Bob.—"Pish! What a sigh is that about a woman! Thou

shalt be Endymion, the nightrake of old, and conquer this shy goddess. Hey, Slang?"

Herewith Slang takes the lead of the conversation, and propounds a plot for running away with the heiress; and I could not help remarking how like the comedy was to life—how the gentlemen always say "thou" and "prythee" and "go to," and talk about heathen goddesses to each other; how their servants are always their particular intimates; how when there is serious love-making between a gentleman and lady, a comic attachment invariably springs up between the valet and the waiting-maid of each; how Lady Grace Gadabout, when she calls upon Rose Ringdove to pay a morning visit, appears in a low satin dress, with jewels in her hair; how Saucebox, her attendant, wears diamond brooches, and rings on all her fingers: while Mrs. Tallyho, on the other hand, transacts all the business of life in a riding-habit, and always points her jokes by a cut of the whip.

This playfulness produced a roar all over the house, whenever it was repeated, and always made our little friends clap their hands and shout in a chorus.

Like that *bon-vivant* who envied the beggars staring into the cookshop windows, and wished he could be hungry, I envied the boys, and wished I could laugh, very much. In the last act, I remember—for it is now very nearly a week ago—everybody took refuge either in a secret door, or behind a screen, or curtain, or under a table, or up a chimney: and the house roared as each person came out from his place of concealment. And the old fellow in top-boots, joining the hands of the young couple (Fitzoffley, of course, pairing off with the widow), gave them his blessing, and thirty thousand pounds.

And ah, ye gods! if I wished before that comedies were like life, how I wished that life was like comedies! Whereon the drop fell; and Augustus, clapping to the opera-glass, jumped up, crying—"Hurray! now for the pantomime."

William Makepeace Thackeray

"An Evening at the Theater,"* from *"Sketches and Travels in London."

4. *Dogb.* First, who think you the most desartless man to be constable?

1. *Watch.* Hugh Oatcake, sir, or George Seacoal; for they can write and read.

Dogb. Come hither, neighbor Seacoal: God hath blest you with a good name: to be a well-favoured man is the gift of fortune; but to write and read comes by nature.

2. *Watch.* Both which, master constable—

Dogb. You have; I knew it would be your answer. Well, for your favour, sir, why, give God thanks, and make no boast of it; and for your writing and reading, let that appear when there is no need of such vanity. You are thought here to be the most senseless and fit man for the constable of the watch; therefore bear you the lantern. This is your charge: you shall comprehend all vagrom men; you are to bid any man stand, in the prince's name.

"Much Ado About Nothing," **Shakespeare**

11 Power in Extemporaneous Speaking

The question of the use of manuscript in speaking before an audience has been widely discust. If it were left to the public, the decision would be unanimously in favor of the extemporaneous style. An audience has a distinct prejudice against a speech or sermon read from a paper. If a speaker refers even to notes, it is considered a point against him. The public expect to see the speaker unencumbered by written notes of any kind. If he has to use them, they conclude he is not master of himself nor of the occasion.

If an address is read from a paper, the listener feels he could as well read it himself at his own home. In the speech or sermon that is read he misses the action of the speaker, the eye to eye communication, the free and spontaneous expression of the voice and body, the direct appeal, the varied pausing, and the infinite shades of modulation attached to extemporaneous delivery. A read speech is likely to be too right-onward in its movement, savoring of the essay, and losing much of the personal element so necessary to effective speaking.

In the early training of a public speaker it is perhaps advisable in most cases to adhere to the manuscript. But as confidence is gained the aim should be to speak entirely without notes of any kind. In these first efforts there should be the most rigid preparation, and in some instances careful memorization. As the speaker gains experience he will find himself more and more able to speak with less detailed preparation, and finally he may be able to do well from merely a clearly defined brief.

Oliver Wendell Holmes said: “The orator—I do not mean the poor slave of a manuscript, who takes his thought chilled and stiffened from its mold, or the impassioned speaker who pours it forth corruscating from the furnace—the orator only becomes our master at the moment when he is himself captured, taken possession of by a sudden rush of fresh inspiration. How well we know the flash of the eye, the thrill of the voice, which are the signature and symbol of nascent thought—thought just entering into consciousness, in which condition, as in the case of the chemist’s elements, it has a combining force at other times wholly unknown.”

This certainly is a plea for the extemporaneous style. This form of address has the advantage of being more conversational and direct than the reading style. It enables the speaker to take constant note of the effect he is producing upon his audience, and to change his method and arrangement to meet unexpected conditions. There is a freshness and a spontaneity about this style that pleases and fascinates an audience, which can not usually be said of the cold made-to-order phraseology of the manuscript speaker. The extemporaneous style gives the speaker unlimited scope for timely observation, the introduction of new illustrations and arguments, for repetition of ideas when required by special circumstances, and numerous other advantages. If the *whole man* should speak, how can this be done if his eyes are glued to a written page?

There is also the question of the vast amount of time that would be saved by the speaker and minister if he could so train himself as not to be obliged to memorize his addresses. Beecher's words regarding the preacher apply also to the average public speaker, who spends days and nights in toil and anxiety over his forthcoming address. Beecher says: "We do not desire to have preaching made less thorough or less instructive, but it is desirable that it should be less burdensome. Many and many a minister is a prisoner all the week to his two sermons. In them he has poured his whole life, and when they are done there is little of him left for pastoral labors and social life. Few men there are who are upborne and carried forward by their sermons. Few men ascend, as the prophet did, in a chariot of fire. The majority of preachers are consciously harnessed, and draw heavily and long at the sermon, which tugs behind them. In every way, then, it is desirable that preaching should be made more easy, that men should learn to take advantage of their own temperament, and that they should learn the best plans and methods."

Henry Ward Beecher was himself the ideal type of extemporaneous speaker. Dr. Wilkinson pays this high tribute to him: "Mr. Beecher's genius had its own elements and its own accompaniments. What are these? One accompaniment was a well-tempered, wonderfully elastic, wonderfully responsive body. This he cared for scrupulously, to maintain it at the highest point of effectiveness. His voice was a living instrument, in native power unsurpassed, and never impaired through ill-health in tile owner. Every muscle of his flesh, every bone and nerve and sinew of his frame, the very blood in throat and cheek and brow, was absolutely obedient to the demand of the orator; and the demand of the orator was immense, for Mr. Beecher's instinct of mimicry was boundless. Prom long habit on Mr. Beecher's part, of absolute command over audiences, his face grew leonine in expression, and the leonine expression itself was constantly more and more a means of such command. Audiences love to be mastered—by a master; and they easily recognize a master by his looks."[1]

It is true that there are some men who can never hope to become successful extemporaneous speakers. These, of course, must continue to use their manuscript, and forego the advantages of the other style. Doctor Storrs tells of his struggle and determination to acquire the ability to speak without notes. He joined a debating society and daring his seminary course did everything he could to advance himself in this way, but with little success. He speaks of his first public efforts to preach without notes as like swimming up the rapids. Then he experimented by having some notes before him, or a "skeleton" of his discourse, but he felt himself worse off than ever. For him, at least, this method proved a failure, obstructing the freedom, freshness, and vigor of his thought. The manuscript in any form, however slight, checked his spontaneity, made him jerky and self-conscious, so that at last he gave himself up wholly to a determined effort to speak entirely without notes of any kind. He refers to the first sermon he preached in Brooklyn thus: "I was called upon unexpectedly for the service, as I was passing through the city, and when I had with me no manuscript sermons. But I had a subject in mind on which I had written not long before, in which I had been at the time much interested, and of which I had made a thorough analysis. The course of thought pursued in the sermon was fresh in my mind, tho the notes were not with me. I preached in a lecture-room, which was wholly filled with attentive hearers. I had no sort of fear of the congregation, which was entirely made up of strangers to me; and I found as I went on, in the treatment of the subject with which I had made myself previously familiar, that the mind worked with a facility, a force, a sense of exhilaration, which I never had in reading from a manuscript I enjoyed the service, and had a certain sense of Christian success in it. The people were interested, and their interest had an instant reflex influence upon my own mind, so that the success became duplicated. It seemed to me, at the end, that it must be always easy and pleasant, under similar conditions, to repeat that experiment"[2]

Not with standing this promising experience, however, the first sermon he preached there, after his installation, was, to use his own words, "nearly a dead failure." Perhaps he had overprepared himself, like the overtrained athlete. There was too much dependence upon verbal memory, and too little upon spontaneous expression. But for sixteen years he persevered and at last was rewarded with the satisfaction of having achieved his long-cherished purpose. These experiences he sets forth most interestingly in the lectures embodied in his book.

In recommending the extemporaneous style of speaking or preaching, too much emphasis can not be placed upon the necessity of the most thorough preparation of the subject matter. There should be the same amount of care and industry and faithfulness as is given to an address intended to be read. The speaker should, indeed, write out his speeches in detail, even tho he does not intend to speak from his notes.

Phillips Brooks does not believe in an arbitrary rule

in this matter. He thinks some men are made for manuscripts, and some for the open platform. "To exclude either class from the ministry," he says, "or to compel either class to use the methods of the other, would rob the pulpit by silencing some of its best men." But according to Cardinal Newman, the manuscript, when used, needs an apology. He says: "While, then, a preacher will find it becoming and advisable to put into writing any important discourse beforehand, he will find it equally a point of propriety and expedience not to read it in the pulpit. I am not of course denying his right to use a manuscript, if he wishes; but he will do well to conceal it, as far as he can, unless, which is the most effectual concealment, whatever be its counterbalancing disadvantages, he prefers, mainly not verbally, to get it by heart To conceal it, indeed, in one way or other, will be his natural impulse; and this very circumstance seems to show us that to read a sermon needs an apology. For, why should he commit it to memory, or conceal his use of it, unless he felt that it was more natural, more decorous, to do without it? And so again, if he employs a manuscript, the more he appears to dispense with it, the more he looks off from it, and directly addresses his audience, the more will he be considered to preach; and, on the other hand, the more will he be judged to come short of preaching the more sedulous he is in following his manuscript line after line, and by the tone of his voice makes it clear that he has got it safely before him. What is this but a popular testimony to the fact that preaching is not reading, and reading is not preaching?"[3]

It must be admitted, then, that the speaker who depends upon a manuscript limits himself in independence and power. The fact that, as Bautain says,

"There are men organized to speak well, as there are birds organized to sing well, bees to make honey, and beavers to build," is not a valid plea for the easier and more comfortable method of reading instead of speaking one's message. Properly done the extemporaneous style at first means increased labor, and greater risk and responsibility, but in the end it will yield the highest possible results in convincing and persuasive speech.

M. de Cormenin gives this stirring advice to French preachers in regard to their congregations: "Take strong hold of their attention. Stir up their pity or indignation, their sympathies, or their pride. Appear to be animated by their breath, all the while you are communicating yours to them. When you have in some degree detached their souls from their bodies and they come and group themselves of their own accord at the foot of the pulpit, riveted beneath the influence of your glance; then da not dally with them, for they are yours, your soul having, as it may be truly said, passed into theirs. Look, now, how they follow its ebb and flow! how they will as you will! how they act as you act! But persist, give them no rest; press your discourse home—and you will soon see all bosoms panting because yours pants; all eyes kindling because yours emit flame, or filling with tears because you grow tender. You will see all the hearers hanging on your lips through the attraction of persuasion; or, rather, you will see nothing, for you yourself will be under the spell of your own emotion; you will bend, you will succumb under your own genius, and you will be more eloquent the less effort you make to appear so."[4]

How can any man thus press his advantage home if his eyes be fixt upon a written manuscript, and having, perhaps, the constant fear that he will "lose his place."

How Incongruous and aimless does it seem in the speaker to gesticulate and twist the body while he is bent over the printed page. The popular ideal of speaking and preaching demands, as has already been said, the eye to eye communication of the speaker, the magnetism of direct appeal, the fire and freedom of the *whole man* unencumbered by manuscript or reading-desk. This was the method generally used by the great Greek and Roman orators and by most of the distinguished speakers of modern times. It is the style of delivery that should be assiduously cultivated by every man aspiring to become a thoroughly proficient public speaker.

REFERENCES

1. William Cleaver Wilkinson, *Masters of Pulpit* Discourse.
2. Richard S. Storrs, Preaching *Without Notes.*
3. John Henry Newman, *Idea of a university.*
4. Quoted by J. Spencer Kennard, D.D., in *Psychic Power in Preaching.*

12 Power in Holding An Audience

It may seem superfluous to say that a public speaker should be heard in order to successfully hold an audience, but it is nevertheless true that many speakers are not heard with ease and satisfaction. This is often due to the habit of speaking through half-closed teeth and mouth. A public speaker should train himself to naturally open his mouth wide enough to give the greatest freedom to his voice and articulation. The long sound of *a* in father and in similar words is frequcntly obscured. This long open position of the mouth is illustrated in the following sentence: Thou art thy father's child.

If the reader will pronounce these words before a looking-glass he will observe the long opening of the mouth necessary to their correct pronunciation. If the correct mouth position in these or any other sounds is modified in the least degree, the pronunciation will be correspondingly incorrect.

In practising distinct enunciation avoid the two extremes of slovenliness and pedantry. Pronunciation, and articulation should never attract the attention of the listener. They should be simply and unobtrusively correct Some one said of a certain preacher: "He speaks so distinctly I do not understand anything he says." The listener's attention was so completely attracted to the manner of speaking that he lost sight of the subject.

For most occasions the speaker will require his chest tones for his public speaking work. This gives fullness, resonance, and depth to utterance; it is less taxing upon the speaker, if combined, as it should be, with abdominal breathing; and it is more agreeable to the listening ear. Head tones are responsible for much of the nasal twang heard on every side, and are largely the cause of weak and sore throats and "Monday-morning prostrations."

A public speaker should cultivate a conversational style of address. The day of stilted and bombastic oratory is passed. Audiences like and demand the most direct kind of speaking possible, and in, words at once simple and idiomatic. Flowery speech, overwrought perorations, and oratorical flights are not now tolerated. This does not imply that intensity, progress, climax, and even a peroration have not their proper place and use, but it does mean that modern taste demands a colloquial style of utterance, adapted to the practical needs of men. Public speaking is merely heightened conversation, and the closer a man keeps to lines of naturalness and simplicity the greater will be his chances of success.

The preacher should be particularly careful not to fall into a certain uniform "tone," or as some one has called it, "a sanctimonious whine," but as a man talking to other men he should always employ a man's voice, use it in a manly style, and project it with manly force and vigor, Intoning, drawling, chanting, monotony and other un-natural tricks of delivery should be studiously avoided, This applies equally to "ministerial tone," singsong, wailing, clipping of consonants, undue prolongation of vowels, and other vocal eccentricities.

A speaker of real power must learn to emphasize his important thoughts, not by mere loudness of voice, nodding of the head, or slapping the hands loudly together, but rather by inflection, change of pitch, judicious pausing, and by other intellectual means. Here, again, the public speaker might take a lesson from the actor who spends hours in careful and painstaking study of the emphasis of a single speech. Intelligent emphasis will do much toward guiding one away from meaningless declamation. It is the best evidence that the speaker knows "what he is talking about."

The beginning of an address or sermon calls for no particular action or gesture. The commencement should be a gradual unfoldment of the speaker's powers, vocal, physical and mental. As he enters more deeply into his thought, some slight gesture may be appropriately used, and changes made in his attitude and standing position. Gesture and action of the body should be used sparingly, however, it being better to use too little than too much. The extremes of standing stock-still or restlessly moving about are to be avoided. No better advice on this subject has ever been given than to "suit the action to the word, the word to the action."

When the speaker stands to address his audience, he should assume a modest and easy attitude, and look his hearers straight in the eyes. The weight of the body should be on the forward part of the foot—not on the heels—the entire foot touching the floor. The knees should be straight In turning from side to side the movements should be made at the waist, not at the neck. The latter give a jerky effect, and impair the freedom of the throat It is advisable at the outset to direct the voice to some one sitting at the back of the room.

When special effects are demanded by the thought, care should be taken not to employ too loud nor too high-keyed a voice, but rather to depend upon increased intensity, roundness, and depth of tone. The voice should be adapted to the size of the room in which one is speaking. When possible it is well to teat the voice there beforehand. This is particularly desirable when one is to speak in an un-usually large auditorium, or in one with which he is not familiar. If there is an echo, or should the audience be unusually scattered, there is special necessity for deliberate and distinct utterance.

In reading from a manuscript or book it should be so held, or placed upon a reading-stand, as to give an un-obstructed view of the speaker's face. Anything that is to be read before an audience, be it sermon, speech, Bible, report, or announcement, should be thoroughly practised aloud in advance.

Once the speaker secures a hold upon his audience this advantage should not be relaxed until the end of his address. The voice may be softened and shaded, as the thought subsides and varies, but the nervous and concentrated energy of the speaker should continue to exercise its powerful control over the audience.

A public speaker will find it advantageous to cultivate a discriminating musical ear. There is the music of speech as there is of song. Symmetrical flaw and rhythm and melody play an important part in fascinating the listener, and give added ease and fluency to the spoken word. Effects of onomatopoeia—words that partly disclose their meaning in their sound—should be studied and intelligently used as elements of effective speech.

Varied thought calls for appropriate and natural variety in speech. A "wriggling" voice is not to be encouraged, nor should the same variety be too often repeated lest it, too, by its very repetition, become monotonous. A just sense of vocal values, of perspective, of modulation adapted to the thought, will best guide the speaker. He will also cultivate lightness of touch. Sounds that come down like a heavy foot soon become burdensome to the ear. The greatest skill and judgment are needed in varying the voice in force, color, key, and flexibility, to properly meet the demands of diversified thought.

The successful speaker should have force in his style. Not merely the force of loudness, but the force of earnestness and sincerity. It is the power behind the man that makes for effective oratory, the power "speaking on the tongue, beaming from the eye, informing every feature, and urging the whole man onward, right onward to his object," this is truly the kind of eloquence to which every worthy public speaker should aspire.

Shrieking emphasis, vehement declamation, startling explosives, stamping the foot, pounding the desk or pulpit, are not evidences of self-possession nor of eloquence, and fail to inspire confidence on the part of the hearer. The carttail orator may harangue and scold his audience, but it is out of place in dignified address.

A deliberate style of speaking is desirable for most occasions. This prevents the crowding of words and obscuring of the thought. Frequent and varied pausing gives dignity and self-possession to the speaker, while at the same time, the hearer has the opportunity of securing clear-cut impressions of his thought. He can follow the speaker with less effort, consequently both his interest and pleasure are enhanced. Deliberateness does not mean a tedious drawing out of sounds or an exaggerated slowness of speech, but an orderly movement in which passes, both grammatical and rhetorical, find their natural and effective place.

The style of speaking insisted upon at our national political conventions offers many valuable suggestions. There the speaker must have something to say, and he must say it briefly. A tedious talker will not be tolerated. The speech must have tact, force, and substance, and it must bear the unmistakable marks of genuineness.

The final test of all public speaking is whether the listener is persuaded to act in accordance with the speaker's views. If, however, the listener's mental resolution to act upon the advice of the speaker evaporates as soon as he is beyond the speaker's voice and influence, the speaking has failed. The speaker must drive home the truth, reenforced by as many suggestions as he can possibly give to the hearer.

Then, again, as referred to in a preceding chapter, there is the personality of the speaker as a force in holding an audience. The greatest power in the world is personal, and as Doctor Bradford says; "Personal power culminates when wisdom and knowledge are married to goodness and love."

A powerful personality will be found then, where brain and heart have been trained in loyal service to others, where a man feels an eager enthusiasm in his work, and where his sympathies are so broad and so deep that they will lead him, if need be, to offer himself a living sacrifice in behalf of his cause.

To maintain his hold upon the people, and to touch

them on all sides, the speaker must be all-round in his taste and development Music, poetry, the drama, science and literature must all have their proper place in his life. How pathetic is this confession of Darwin:

"Up to the age of thirty or beyond it, poetry of many kinds gave me great pleasure; and even as a schoolboy I took intense delight in Shakespeare, especially in the historical plays. I have also said that pictures formerly gave me considerable and music very great delight. But now for many years I can not endure to read a line of poetry. I have tried lately to read Shakespeare, and found it so intolerably dull that it nauseated me. I have also almost lost my taste for pictures or music... My mind seems to have become a kind of machine for grinding general laws out of large collections of facts; but why this should have caused the atrophy of that part of the brain alone, on which the higher tastes depend, I can not conceive... If I had to live my life again, I would have made a rule to read some poetry and listen to some music; at least once every week; for perhaps the parts of my brain now atrophied would thus have been kept alive through use. The loss of these tastes is a loss of happiness, and may possibly be injurious to the intellect, and more probably to the moral character, by enfeebling the emotional part of our nature."

A public speaker can not hope to be successful in holding an audience without a deep-seated and well-directed sympathetic nature. "The secret of lasting success," says a writer, "in social conversation, in platform speech, in pulpit sermon, is sympathy, *sympathy*, SYMPATHY. In the public speaker and the private speaker, there should ever be sympathy for class or for mass, for the family or for the individual."

The speaker should have a definite purpose in view. There can be little power or satisfactory result in haphazard effort. He should know whether he is merely to entertain, or to instruct, convince, and persuade. Much will depend upon the occasion. A pulpit address will differ materially from an after-dinner speech, and what would he appropriate in a court of law, or in a scientific disquisition, might be uninteresting and out of place before a popular audience.

It is said that in a certain tribe of savages a man is allowed to speak at their councils only so long as he can stand on one foot When the other toe touches the ground his time is up. What a relief this would be at times to some of our own long-suffering audiences!

A public speaker should be careful not to exceed his time limit Many an otherwise admirable address has been ruined by being too long drawn out. It is dangerous to be too discursive, to succumb to the temptation to add "one more story." The old-time "Finally," "Lastly," "In conclusion," "One word more and I have done" have proved a pitfall to many a public speaker. It is an art to know how to successfully end a speech, to finish well within the prescribed time, and to leave your audience before they leave you.

13 Power in Prayer

There is an inexhaustible power and efficacy in prayer, known only to those who have faithfully practised it. The praying that is done in secret will materially affect the style of one's public prayer. But whatever the form may be, this is true: "Who rises from prayer a better man, his prayer is answered."

Spurgeon in one of his addresses to his students says that prayer should be marked by solemnity, humility, and reverence. He deprecates long prayers. Frequent repetition and hackneyed expressions are to be avoided. One should cultivate a heavenly attitude of mind in prayer. God is to be entreated, not commanded. The eyes should he closed, that the Lord alone may be the object of prayer. Sickening superabundance of endearing words, and rhetorical display, have no place in earnest and effective prayer.

Learning to pray is like learning to do anything else. It comes from diligent practise. The question is sometimes asked by divinity students to what extent public prayer should be prepared in advance. No general rule can be laid down for this, as so much depends upon circumstances. There should be, however, in every case, a preparation of the heart, in which actual words may not be committed to memory, but in which the general ideas of the prayer have been thought out and arranged in order in the mind. Unseeming hesitation in public prayer, lack of appropriate words, and discursiveness, sometimes robs prayer of real effectiveness. Spontaneity, sincerity, tenderness, and God-wardness are some of the characteristics of devout and heartfelt prayer.

The great preachers of the world have recognized the supreme power of prayer. In speaking of Dr. Russell H. Conwell, the Baptist divine, of Philadelphia, a writer says: "He is a man of prayer and a man of work. Loving, great-hearted, unselfish, cheery, practical, hard-working, he yet draws his greatest inspiration from that silent inner communion with the Master he serves with such single-hearted, unfaltering devotion."

This is Dr. Conwell's own tribute to prayer: "There is planted in every human heart this knowledge, namely, that there is a power beyond our reach, a mysterious potency shaping the forces of life, which if we would win we must have in our favor. There come to us all events over which we have no control by physical or mental power. Is there any hope of guiding those mysterious forces? Yes, friends, there is a way of securing them in our favor or preventing them from going against us. How? It is by prayer. When a man has done all he can do, still there is a mighty, mysterious agency over which he needs influence to secure success. The only way he can reach that is by prayer."

Prayer must be earnest, a thing of the heart It should not be a thing of the Up, of formality, of a wandering mind. It should be real, soaring, confident—prayer such as this is a great force in personal power.

Thomas Guthrie, in his touching sermon, "The

Necessity and Power of Prayer," says: "Child of God! pray on. By prayer thy hand can touch the stars, thy arm stretch up to heaven. Nor let thy holy boldness be dashed by the thought that prayer has no power to bend these skies, and bring down thy God. When I pull on the rope which fastens my frail and little boat to a distant and mighty ship, if my strength can not draw its vast bulk to me, I can draw myself to it—to ride in safety under the protection of its guns; to enjoy in want the fullness of its stores. And it equally serves my purpose, and supplies my needs, that prayer, altho it were powerless to move God to me, moves me to God. If He does not descend to earth, I—as it were—ascend to heaven."

Where can we find better advice upon the subject of prayer than in the Bible itself? Here we read:

"Thou, when thou prayest, enter into thy closet, and when thou hast shut thy door, pray to thy Father which is in secret, and thy Father which seeth in secret shall reward thee openly. But when ye pray, use not vain repetitions, as the heathen do; for they think that they shall be heard for their much speaking. Be not ye therefore like unto them for your Father knoweth what things ye have need of, before ye ask him. After this manner therefore pray ye: Our Father which art in heaven, Hallowed be thy name. Thy kingdom come. Thy will be done in earth, as it is in heaven. Give us this day our daily bread. And forgive us our debts, as we forgive our debtors. And lead us not into temptation, but deliver us from evil: for thine is the kingdom, and the power, arid the glory, forever. Amen." (*Matt,* vi., 6-13.)

"The sacrifice of the wicked is an abomination to the Lord: but the prayer of the upright is his delight" (*Prov.* *xv*, 1.)

"And Jesus said unto them, Because of your unbelief: for verily I say unto you, if ye have faith as a grain of mustard seed, ye shall say unto this mountain, Remove hence to yonder place; and it shall remove; and nothing shall be impossible unto you." (*Matt,* xvii., 20.)

"Pray for them which despitefully use you, and persecute you." (*Matt,* v., 44.)

"Watch and pray, that ye enter not into temptation." (*Matt,* xxvi., 41.)

"What things soever ye desire, when ye pray, believe that ye receive them, and ye shall have them," (*Mark* xi., 24.)

"Take ye heed, watch and pray: for ye know not when the time is." (*Mark* xiii., 33.)

"Men ought always to pray, and not to faint." (*Luke* xviii., 1.)

"We know not what we should pray for as we ought: but the Spirit itself, maketh intercession for us with groanings which can not be uttered." (*Bom.* viii., 26.)

"I will pray with the spirit, and I will pray with the understanding also." (I *Cor.* xiv., 15.)

"Pray without ceasing." (I *Thess.* v., 17.)

"I will therefore that men pray everywhere, lifting up holy hands, without wrath and doubting." (*I Tim. ii,* 8.)

"Is any among you afflicted? let him pray." (*James* v., 13.)

"Praying always with all prayer and supplication in the Spirit." (*Eph.* vi., 18.)

"And being in an agony he prayed more earnestly." (*Luke* xxii., 44.)

"Elias was a man subject to like passions as we are, and he prayed earnestly that it might not rain: and it rained not on the earth by the space of three years and six months." (*James* v., 17.)

"But we will now give ourselves continually to prayer, and to the ministry of the word." (*Acts* vi., 4.)

"Be careful for nothing; but in every thing by prayer and supplication with thanksgiving let your requests be made known unto God." (*Phil,* iv., 6.)

"And the prayer of faith shall save the sick, and the Lord shall raise him up; and if he have committed sins, they shall be forgiven." (*James* v., 15.)

"Confess your faults one to another, and pray one for another, that ye may be healed. The effectual fervent prayer of a righteous man availeth much." (*James* v., 16.)

Prayer, then, should be founded upon faith and earnestness. We must avoid vain repetition or doubting, and with thanksgiving and confidence make our requests known unto God. We should pray often, not only for ourselves but for one another, fervently, believingly, both with the spirit and the understanding. Such prayers, especially from one that is righteous, will avail much, such prayers can not fail to be a source of real power.

The Rev. Louis Albert Banks, in his suggestive book, "Windows for Sermons," speaking of genuine prayer, says:

"One of the greatest secrets of effective prayer is that the attitude of the heart shall be right toward God. The heart that recognizes the divine wisdom and love and trusts to them will pray as simply as a child asking help from its mother. One of the most beautiful prayers I have ever read is that of Fenelon. 'O Lord! I know not what I should ask of Thee. Thou knowest only what I want; and Thou lovest me, if I am Thy friend, better than I can love myself. O Lord! give to me, Thy child, what is proper, whatsoever it may be. I dare not ask either crosses or comforts. I only present myself before Thee. I open my heart to Thee. Behold my wants, which I myself am ignorant of; but do Thou behold, and do, according to Thy mercy, smite or Heal, depress me or raise me up. I adore all Thy purposes without knowing them. I am silent; I offer myself in sacrifice. I abandon myself to Thee. I have no more desire but to accomplish Thy will. Lord, teach me how to pray. Dwell Thou Thyself in me by the Holy Spirit *Amen.*' "

In public prayer the minister uses his supremest faculty, that of communion with God. He speaks on behalf of his people, and must voice their needs and sentiments. His language should be simple and fitting, and his sympathies large enough to include all. It will be seen, therefore, that prayer is too important a matter to be left to the chance of the moment. It demands the same care and thought and meditation as are given to the preparation of the sermon.

The style and manner of public prayer are suggested by Professor Schenck in these words: "Terms of familiarity and endearment should be avoided, since we are addressing the Infinite and Holy God. Simple and chaste language should be used, easily understood by the ignorant and distrest and also proper to use before the throne of the Most High. The tone of the voice should be easily heard by all, from the first word of the prayer to the last, and should be earnest but never loud nor boisterous, since God is near by and loves to hear His people pray. The posture should be reverent; usually the minister should stand with claspt hands, without gesture, and the people should listen with bowed heads."

The criticism is often made that public prayer is too general and does not meet the specific needs of people. Spurgeon speaks of this generalization in prayer as disastrous. He pleads for definite prayer, asking clearly and distinctly for certain mercies. "If a regiment of soldiers should all fire off their guns anyhow, possibly somebody might be killed, but the majority of the enemy would be missed." So, in prayer, the speaker should have a target at which he aims, a clearly defined purpose on behalf of his people. In this way public prayer may be made a source of infinite power to both minister and congregation.

14 Power in Silence and Repose

Paradoxical tho it may seem, there is an eloquence and a power in silence which every speaker should seek to cultivate. A man who knows how and when to listen is not only open to increase his store of knowledge, but will often receive credit for wisdom he does not really possess. The habit of silence gives time for necessary meditation and for accumulating power for subsequent use. It makes one acquainted with the inner life. It is the most direct means of developing spiritual power.

A silent man is usually a thinking man. He takes time to think, to test his ideas before giving them expression, to formulate his thought into clear and logical sequence. He obeys the admonition to "Think before you speak," consequently his thoughts when exprest carry weight because of their clearness and maturity. There are far too few of these silent men who take time to think, and too many who talk first and think afterward.

Cardinal Newman doubtless had in mind this lack of genuine thinking when he said: "What is more common than the sight of grown men, talking on political or moral or religious subjects, in that offhand, idle way, which we signify by the word *unreal?* 'That they simply do not know what they are talking about,' is the spontaneous silent remark of any man of sense who hears them. Hence such persons have no difficulty in contradicting themselves in successive sentences without being conscious of it Hence others, whose defect in intellectual training is more latent, have their most unfortunate crotchets, as they are called, or hobbies, which deprive them of the influence which their estimable qualities would otherwise secure. Hence others can never look straight before them, never see the point, and have no difficulties in the most difficult subjects. Others are hopelessly obstinate and prejudiced, and, after they have been driven from their opinions, return to them the next moment without even an attempt to explain why. Others are so intemperate and intractable that there is no greater calamity for a good cause than that they should get hold of it."

Too much introspection and meditation may make one morbid, but intelligent self-analysis, reasonably pursued, is necessary to the highest growth. Periods of silence and relaxation offer the best conditions for this work and study. When one thinks of the noise and nervousness of modern city life, of the "bottled-lightning quality of Americana," it is reasonable to assume that only by carefully planned times for silence and quiet meditation can one hope to develop the highest and best in one's spiritual nature.

The knowledge gathered in these moments of silence, if properly applied, brings one into more intimate touch with the truth. A man finds out what things weaken his power, as well as what things contribute to it, and he can, if he will, change from destructive to constructive effort. With this new knowledge comes increased responsibility, but there comes, too, increased pleasure in the work of readjustment and of self-mastery.

The practise of silence brings reserve power, and poise, by which a man trains himself to be equal to emergencies as they arise. In this listening attitude he hears whisperings from secret spiritual sources that otherwise could not be discerned. It is from these moments that he draws his deepest and moat enduring inspiration. Every man has his own individual mind-world to explore. No one else can possibly do it for him. Its infinite possibilities must remain unrealized and undeveloped unless he is in some way led to do this work for himself.

Through relaxation and repose a man rests his physical and mental machinery, generates unsuspected energy, and at the moment of need is conscious of new and vastly increased power. To learn to "let go," to thoroughly relax both mind and body, usually requires patient and persistent practise. In the end it will repay the student many-fold in increased health and self-control.

Many persons waste valuable energy in unnecessary muscular contraction. They frown in reading a newspaper, sit anxiously in a car as if to help it to its destination, or at night they endeavor to hold the bed up lest it fall to pieces. Many times each hour they expend their power in such useless habits as clenching the fist, drumming with the fingers or tapping with the foot, biting the lips, rocking the body, or indulging in needless anxiety, anger or other excitement. These habits are a constant drain upon even the strongest constitutions, and eventually lead to physical and mental impoverishment and sometimes to nervous prostration.

Relaxation and repose act as a soothing influence

to the nerves. They take the tension off the mental machinery, rest the body, and restore a man to his normal condition. As a man gradually forms this habit of doing his work without tension, he finds he can accomplish more and better work than he ever did before. It is this freedom from nerve-destroying contraction and anxiety that Carlyle has in mind when he says:

"Give us, oh, give us the man who sings at his work! He will do more in the same time—he will do it better—he will persevere longer. One is scarcely sensible of fatigue whilst he marches to music. The very stars are said to make harmony as they revolve in their spheres. Wondrous is the strength of cheerfulness, altogether past calculation in its powers of endurance. Efforts, to be permanently useful, must be uniformly joyous, a spirit all sunshine, graceful from very gladness, beautiful because bright."

Ruskin says: "All one's life is a music if one touches the notes rightly and in time—but there must be no hurry." The story of the creation—six days labor and then *rest*— is a rebuke to the ceaseless heart-breaking pace of the average American. "You wear too much expression on your faces," said Dr. Clouston, a Scottish medical man, in speaking of Americans. "You are living like an army with all its reserves engaged in action. The duller countenances of the British population betoken a better scheme of life. They suggest stores of reserved nervous force to fall back upon, if any occasion should arise that requires it This inexeitability, this presence at all times of power not used, I regard as the great safeguard of our British people. The other thing in you gives me a sense of insecurity, and you ought somehow to tone yourselves down. You really do carry too much expression, you take too intensely the trivial moments of life."

A mental attitude of calmness may be brought about by realizing the positive injury that is being done by contracted muscles. The mind should be emptied as far as possible of all disturbing thoughts, such as fear, worry, resentment, and anger. The reader may experiment at once by allowing the hand and arm to relax at the side or wherever it may fall It should be made to feel as heavy as lead—not held down, but down because of its own weight This "limp" attitude may be gradually extended to other parts of the body, until finally one may lie down and give oneself up completely to the comfortable feeling of repose and relaxation. A wonderful power and facility will come after a little practise.

RELAXATION EXERCISES

The following exercises may be practised for a few minutes daily:

1. Lie down. Hake yourself limp and passive. Lightly toss one hand in the air, and allow it to drop of its own weight where it will. Repeat with the other hand. Then do the same with the legs, one at a time. Raise the head and let it drop. Roll the body over from side to side, allowing the arms, legs and head to fall where they like. In a few minutes the entire body should become thoroughly relaxed. It will greatly assist at first to cultivate a lazy or drowsy feeling in doing this exercise.

2. Now rest the mind along with your relaxed body, still lying down. Learn to "let go" all mental strain. Gently direct the mind in turn to the feet, arms, head, back, throat, stomach, knees, abdomen, heart, and tongue. Do this very slowly and patiently. Then combine with this exercise

thoughts of health, and ease, and power. You will be surprised at the feeling of rest and renewed energy that you will shortly experience.

3. Stand erect. Droop the head and shoulders. Shake the body thoroughly, while relaxed as much as possible, allowing the arms to go loosely where they may.

4. Support yourself on one foot by holding a chair. Vigorously shake the other leg. Reverse.

5. While standing, relax both arms and shake them vigorously. Repeat with the hands alone.

6. Sit in a chair. Relax the arms, head and waist. Gradually let go of the entire body. Make the feet to rest heavily on the floor. Assume a feeling of drowsiness.

7. Walk around the room, with body, head, and arms relaxed, in imitation of intoxication.

8. Drop gently forward to one knee, then to the other, then to one hand, and to the other, then let the whole body drop to the floor. These movements should be done slowly, without jarring of any kind.

9. Hold the arm at the side, bent at the elbow, and rapidly vibrate it up and down so as to shake the head and upper body. Then relax thoroughly. Repeat with the other arm.

10. With arm extended straight out at side, palm of the hand down, rapidly vibrate the arm up and down. Then relax and repeat with the other arm.

11. Sit as perfectly still as you can, relaxed, for two minutes.

12. Stand as still as possible for one minute.
13. Stand on tiptoe, reach as high as you can with your hands, tense the whole body until it trembles, then slowly relax into a sitting position on a chair. Repeat several times, each time relaxing a little longer.
14. While walking, inhale slowly and rhythmically, mentally counting ten to ten steps, then slowly and evenly exhale in the same way. Avoid jerking the breaths. They should be slow and even.
15. Inhale deeply, filling out the chest and abdomen to their fullest capacity, then gently and slowly relax as you completely exhale.